Motivated *IN* Minutes

1,001 Tips & Ideas to Help You Get MOTIVATED

JASON GRACIA

GRACIA ENTERPRISES
Madison Wisconsin

To the children of BGA.

You have taught me more than I will ever
be able to teach you.

✦ ✦ ✦

Design and compositon by John Reinhardt Book Design
Internal Clipart: NVTech

Library of Congress Cataloging-in-Publication Data

Gracia, Jason
   Motivated in Minutes
   ISBN: 0-9714733-1-5

   Library of Congress Catalog Number 2002091429

   Reference: Motivation, Management

   ISBN # 0-9714733-1-5

First Printing June 2002

Printed in the United States

Published by Gracia Enterprises, Madison, Wisconsin

Contents

Section III: Attitude

Section IV: Online and Offline Learning

Appendix A: Resources

Introduction

IMAGINE A RACE WITH SIX RUNNERS. On a clear afternoon, they took their marks at the starting blocks. As far as anyone could tell, each runner seemed to be in good physical shape and capable of running a strong race. On the surface, it looked to be anyone's event.

Upon further examination, however, you would see that this was very far from the truth. The runners were not equal, nor were they all capable of completing the race. Only one had what it took to be successful, and only one crossed the finish line.

When the gunshot sounded, the first runner, after covering only a short distance, stopped and left the race. This runner was indifferent. He told others that he wanted to run, and he even told himself that winning the race was his goal. The truth was, he didn't have the desire necessary to create motivation.

The second runner didn't move when the race began. This runner was in doubt. Because he didn't believe that he could be successful, he didn't risk taking part in the race. He lacked the belief that was necessary for motivation.

The third runner couldn't get his legs to move quite right. Instead of running a race, he tripped over his own feet. This runner was uninformed about the sport and technique of running. Without knowing how to run, he couldn't last very long. He lacked the knowledge necessary for motivation.

The fourth runner showed up late for the race, and when it began, he ran in the wrong direction. This runner was unprepared for the race. He didn't know where he was going, and didn't have a chance of accidentally bumping into the finish line. He lacked the goals necessary for motivation.

The fifth runner glanced around, hesitated, and ran into the locker room. He was afraid; afraid of looking foolish in front of others and he was afraid to fail. He lacked the confidence necessary for motivation. The sixth runner was strong, fast, and athletic. He loved to run, believed he could win, knew the proper techniques, had a goal, and was confident and unafraid of failing. When the race began, he flew down the track and won the race in record time. The sixth runner had every quality necessary to be motivated.

This simple story illustrates the major reasons why people are not motivated. When you find yourself in this state, you are either: indifferent, doubtful, uninformed, unprepared, or afraid. The great news is, there are steps you can take to overcome each of these obstacles.

That's why this book was written, to offer you 1,001 tips, ideas, and techniques to help you find where your desires lie, believe in your abilities, gain the knowledge necessary for success, set powerful and effective goals, and use failing to your advantage. In short, this book will help you gain control over each obstacle to motivation, allowing you to get what you want, when you want it.

Inside you'll find three sections focused on motivation, goals, and attitude. With an understanding of these areas you will create a complete picture of what it takes to gain and maintain motivation. The tips will take you step-by-step through the process of finding what you want, creating a plan to get it, and staying motivated and positive until the end.

Along with these sections, you'll find many extras throughout the book. There are several chapters dedicated to showing parents or coaches how to help others get motivated, set goals, and improve their attitudes. To get you started on the right path, you will find a goal program to help you create a concrete plan for the future. The plan covers your health, wealth, career, relationships, and personal achievement. Several of the tips inside direct you to particular organizations or businesses, and to make this process easier for you, a resource section has been included in the back of the book.

When you know how to motivate yourself, every aspect of your life can be exactly as you want it. You will have the tools to improve your health, relationships, wealth, career, and happiness. Motivation is the key to getting from where you are now, to where you want to be. You now have 1,001 tips to get you started.

SECTION ONE
Motivation

1

Motivation 1, 2, 3!

WHAT YOU NEED TO SUCCEED is already in you. The key is getting that knowledge and skill out of your head and into action. The tips inside will help you get excited about making some long overdo changes in your life, as well as little improvements along the way.

The ideas are quick and easy, and can help you become motivated in no time at all. Many times in our lives we know what we should do, but can't find the energy or will to get moving. Soon you'll have more than enough ways to take care of that problem.

Special Olympics Volunteer

Get involved as a coach, judge, or event volunteer for the Special Olympics. Spending time with others to help them achieve goals and dreams they never thought possible is a great way to give back and get motivated.

The Time to Wait is Over

"I'll get started when the kids are out of school." "I'll do it when the kids go back to school." "I'll wait until the time is right." The time and situation will never be perfect. Putting off your goals and dreams until everything is in place may leave you waiting for the rest of your life. Time keeps moving even if you do not. If you have the ability to begin work on your goals today, don't wait until tomorrow.

✦ ✦ ✦

Travel

A change of pace will motivate you. If you stay in one place too long, you begin to take things for granted and settle into a dangerous level of comfort. Simply by visiting a neighboring state you will see things you've never seen before, and meet people you have never had the opportunity to meet. There is a whole world outside your door, waiting to be explored.

✦ ✦ ✦

Draw the Picture

There are many ways to bring ideas from your head into a more concrete form. Drawing is a simple, quick, and inexpensive way to do this. Why is it important? Creativity is key to motivation. Drawing is action. It is making an intangible thought tangible. In other words, it is taking a good idea and making it real.

✦ ✦ ✦

Paint

A bit more supplies, but the effect is just the same. Grab your brush, easel, and your mind.

Have fun creating new images or recreating scenes from your surroundings. In this case, artistic ability doesn't matter and shouldn't hold you back from giving it a try. You can even create twice as much motivation by painting a picture that you find personally inspiring.

✦ ✦ ✦

Speak

Communicate with those around you. It could be a paid performance in front of hundreds of inspired listeners, or a group of friends eager to hear about your thoughts on a particular subject. When you speak to others about your ideas, you will be solidifying your own beliefs. The best way to learn about something is to teach it to someone else.

✦ ✦ ✦

It All Starts with a Goal

Set goals. This is a key aspect of motivation. Nearly every successful individual makes goals an integral part of their life. If you want to achieve greater happiness and success, you must do the same. In the later sections of the book you will find hundreds of tips and techniques to help you set effective goals and accomplish every one of them.

✦ ✦ ✦

People Have Done More, With Less

Remember this every time you feel like the cards are stacked against you, or you don't have what it takes to make it. You not only have what it takes, but you most likely have more than what thousands of other successful people had before you. With much less

Patience and perseverance have a magical effect before which difficulties disappear and obstacles vanish.

John Quincy Adams

Write

Getting all of your thoughts onto paper is calming, motivating, and will give you some fresh ideas to work with. It doesn't matter how or what you write, just that you spend time writing. Here are a few ideas to help you get started:

✧ write a short story
✧ write an autobiographical story
✧ write an essay
✧ write a letter to a friend

than what we enjoy today, people have created lives of health, wealth, success, and happiness.

✦ ✦ ✦

The Best of the Best

Study the lives of those who have inspired millions of people throughout the world. Learning about the lives of ordinary individuals accomplishing extraordinary things will inspire and motivate you to success and happiness. With a little research you can find stories that relate to the challenges you are facing in your life. These stories can serve as a blueprint for your plan. Several individuals include Mother Theresa, Gandhi, Beethoven, Michelangelo, and Ben Franklin.

✦ ✦ ✦

Improve Your Attitude

You must have the right attitude before real change and improvement can take place. Along the way you will no doubt run into obstacles and setbacks. With a positive attitude you will see these as small, temporary challenges and be able to keep progressing without becoming weighed down with stress and worry.

✦ ✦ ✦

Motivation Station

We all have movies that motivate us or make us want to reach for more. Make a collection of these movies and create your own motivation station. Whenever you are in need of a quick boost, and have two hours to spare, you'll have just the perfect solution.

✦ ✦ ✦

Articles for Motivation

Compile articles that you find personally motivating or inspiring. Newspapers, magazines, and books contain thousands of stories that cover the spectrum of motivational material. When you find a great article file it away for future reference.

✦ ✦ ✦

Motivate Others

When you help others, they will in turn be helping you. If a friend or family member is in need of a little motivation, make it your personal goal to help them achieve success. Motivating your friend will help you to learn about motivation from a whole different viewpoint.

✦ ✦ ✦

Motivational Places

Make a list of places that you find motivating. This could include the local park, mountains, the countryside, or a personal spot that holds meaning for you. Some of your best thinking will take place there.

✦ ✦ ✦

Motivational E-zines

Subscribe to motivational newsletters online. They are called E-zines and are usually delivered to your electronic mailbox every two weeks. They are free, informative, and unsubscribing is easy. There are thousands of electronic newsletters so you'll easily be able to find a few good ones that suit your needs.

✦ ✦ ✦

Through perseverance many people win success out of what seemed destined to be certain failure.

Benjamin Disraeli

The Renaissance Man

Take time to study art, literature, history, and philosophy. When you do, you'll learn about some of the greatest thinkers the world has ever known. Studying about the lives of men and women who have shaped our world will motivate you to live your life better.

Print Out E-zines

Print out your favorite electronic newsletters. Information can pile up very quickly on your computer and can easily be lost or accidentally deleted. Printing out valuable resources will ensure that this doesn't happen to you. When you come across a great newsletter, print it out and file the newsletter into a folder or binder. Along with newsletters focused on motivation, you can create files for goals, attitude, and any other area in which you are interested.

✦ ✦ ✦

Find a Role Model

Find a mentor or role model. After a little poking around you will find a person who has personal experience that can help you in your endeavors. Simply listening to old stories or advice is enough to make the process worthwhile. Don't reinvent the wheel. Find others who are willing to share and listen to what they have to say.

✦ ✦ ✦

Become a Mentor

The teacher learns as much, if not more, than the student. Only when you explain ideas to others do you really understand the subject. That is why mentoring someone else is an excellent way to get motivated. You can join a group that is focused on mentoring, or help your friends and family with challenges they are facing.

✦ ✦ ✦

Motivational Web Sites

Using any of the popular search engines search the Internet for *motivation*. Your search will retrieve millions of pages containing some type of link to motivation. Within these you will find a few gems. Free information is among the best information.

✦ ✦ ✦

Print Online Articles

When you read an article that you enjoy, print it. Many times people say to themselves, "This is a great article, I should save it," but after a few days it is forgotten and erased. Because of this, a great deal of valuable information is lost. You will no doubt find many interesting articles while looking through the Web sites. Print out the articles and file them into a folder or binder.

✦ ✦ ✦

Share the Articles

Share the lessons you have learned with other people. If you go to a Web site with a great story, tell your brother, sister, mother, father, uncle, aunt, neighbors, or friends about it. Explain the article in your own words. This will allow the ideas to sink in. When you learn something, and then talk about it to other people, you are giving the information a chance to become set in your mind. You will retain the information you have just learned.

✦ ✦ ✦

Clean Your Thinking Space

Take twenty minutes to clean your thinking spot. If you do your best thinking in the den,

Do not confuse motion and progress. A rocking horse keeps moving but does not make any progress.

Alfred A. Montapert

Create Individual Idea Notebooks

Purchase three to five notebooks and designate each one for a particular area of your life. Writing down your ideas and solutions in a notebook is very beneficial, and this is a simple way to make the process more organized and efficient. You could create a notebook for:

- ✧ work ideas
- ✧ ideas to help at home
- ✧ personal goals or objectives

make sure that room is organized and uncluttered. A disorganized environment will create a disorganized mind. A clean environment will make for crisp and focused thinking.

✦ ✦ ✦

Write Out Your Excuses

Make a written list of the reasons you normally use for not doing something that you should, or want, to do. At this time it doesn't matter if they are legitimate or simply excuses. Think of all the areas of your life: health, wealth, happiness, and success. If you are not working as diligently as you should be, what's your reason?

✦ ✦ ✦

Why Don't They Work?

Next to each item on your list, brainstorm for solutions. For example, if you wrote down that you put off your goal because you have a full-time job, you could write that you still have five to six hours per night to work on your tasks after work. Some reasons are actually valid. Next to these items write out how you are going to work around these obstacles.

✦ ✦ ✦

Be Honest With Yourself

When listing reasons and excuses for procrastination, be honest with yourself. You won't get anywhere if you spend your time defending your lack of action. Realize that you have put things off and write out the logical response to each.

✦ ✦ ✦

To-Do Lists

Create a task list on Sunday night that covers the upcoming week's goals or tasks. Even if you don't think you'll have the motivation to do a certain project, list it. Your list will keep you up to date on responsibilities and keep you aware of your goals. Keep the list close to you for reference. Make different columns or use different colored pens to denote the importance of each item.

✦ ✦ ✦

Unfinished Items

Move incomplete tasks to the top of tomorrow's list. This will guarantee that each item will be finished even if time runs out on its scheduled date. If you find that items are consistently being moved to the top of the next day's list, you may have to reduce your workload.

✦ ✦ ✦

Have a Plan

Create a plan for your future. Where do you want to be in five years? Ten years? What steps are you going to take to get there? When you have a plan you will see opportunities where you didn't before. If your plan is to start a small business, and you hear of a visiting seminar focusing on that area, you would most likely attend. Without your plan, the seminar would have been ignored.

✦ ✦ ✦

Motivation through Technology

Purchase electronic devices to help with motivation. If you are trying to get in shape you

Even if you are on the right track, you'll get run over if you just sit there.

Will Rogers

It's Everywhere

Keep your eyes open for motivation. Motivating stories are in every newspaper and magazine. Many television shows offer tips and ideas to help you live a better life. Talking with friends can reveal to you motivational techniques that you never thought of. Become aware of the world around you and you will find advice and information around every corner.

- ❖ stories in newspapers
- ❖ books
- ❖ television shows
- ❖ talks with a friend
- ❖ observing what you see

can use distance meters and pedometers to measure your success. All of your motivation and progress doesn't have to come from within, although that should be the bulk of your drive. Look into gadgets that may help you stay motivated.

✦ ✦ ✦

Create Your Own Luck

When you use luck as the reason for your failure or success, you are giving up your control. Saying things like, "When I fail, it's just bad luck," or, "Life just wasn't fair." is flawed and negative thinking. You create your own luck by making smart decisions and working hard. You are in control.

✦ ✦ ✦

Extra! Extra!

Write a headline about your life for your own fictitious newspaper. 'John Doe graduates from college, goes on to save lives as a doctor!' Picture the paper going out to millions of subscribers around the globe. After your paper has been printed, it's your job to make the headlines true. You can even write the headline on a sheet of paper for a reminder.

✦ ✦ ✦

Make it a Game

Make chores or tasks into a game. Games are fun, challenging, and motivating. This tip works especially well with smaller tasks such as getting out of bed early, cleaning the house, or washing the car. When you face a situation like this, make a game out of it and have fun. See how long it takes you to clean a certain room. Try to beat your time in the next room. Simple games like this will help you get started and allow you to complete hundreds of tasks and chores.

+ + +

Visual Motivation

Put up a picture of your role model or mentor. You can find these in magazines, newspapers, or on the Internet. If you want to take it a step further, write to them and ask for an autographed photo. Keeping a picture of the man or woman whom you respect is a great way to stay motivated.

+ + +

Diploma Goes Here

If you have received a high school, college, graduate school, or other type of degree or accreditation, place it prominently on your desk or wall. This is not to show off your accomplishments to others, but to remind you of what can be achieved with hard work and dedication.

+ + +

How Many Targets Do You See?

Your goal is to hit the bull's-eye of the target in front of you. One target, one goal, one focus. Then, out of nowhere, a new target appears, the target of self-doubt, "What if you miss? You'll look like a fool!" Soon, more targets pop up as you begin to question yourself and your ability. Soon you have a hundred targets swaying back and forth and you can't decide where to shoot. You don't know what to do. Don't let fear and self-doubt cloud your focus and judgment. Zero in on your goal, take aim, and hit your target.

Motivation is like food for the brain. You cannot get enough in one sitting. It needs continual and regular top up's.

Peter J. Davies

Success Stories

Print out, write down, or tape record stories you hear that inspire or motivate you. If you read an article about a local man overcoming cancer, save it. If you read a magazine article about a mountain climber born without legs, rip it out and keep it. If they could grab your attention once, chances are they will do it again. Place your hard-copies in a file folder or binder. Here are a few places to look:

✧ magazines
✧ newspapers
✧ newsletters
✧ television specials
✧ talking with others
✧ your own story

You Are Never Too Old

Regardless of your age, you can accomplish almost anything. Men and women have started their lives in their sixties and seventies, and many more will continue to do so. Don't let your age be a factor in your willingness to give it a try.

✦ ✦ ✦

You Are Never Too Young

It doesn't matter how young you are, people who are even younger have done more. If you have a great idea, then do it. If you want to follow a dream, then follow it. The number of years you have been on this Earth should not determine what you can and cannot achieve.

✦ ✦ ✦

Tomorrow isn't Guaranteed

Make the most of your time because you never know when it will be up. If you continue to put things off until tomorrow, you may never get a chance to do them at all. Life is short. Make sure you enjoy every last minute of it.

✦ ✦ ✦

Make a Round Tuit

"When are you going back to school?" "When are you going to start working out?" "When are you going to start writing your first novel?" These questions are often answered with, "When I get around to it." The time for the *Round Tuit* is here. Cut out a circle from construction paper or plastic, and place the word Tuit (pronounced to-it) on the front in big, bold letters. Keep your round tuit handy as a constant reminder for motivation.

The Right Side of the Bed

Create a morning routine that contains the things you enjoy. I get up early, get a muffin and a newspaper from the corner store, and read the latest events before I start work. This never fails to get me started in just the right way. A great start to your day will help to make for an even better finish.

✦ ✦ ✦

A Change of Pace

Get up one hour earlier than usual once a week. This will let you take your time in the morning without rushing through the routine. Make breakfast, read the newspaper, or walk the dog. This is an easy to way to bring calm and relaxation to your life. If you have enough time, go for a morning run in your neighborhood.

✦ ✦ ✦

New Year's Resolution

Make a New Year's Resolution each year. This national pastime would be a great idea if it weren't for one small problem; no one sticks to it. There are many reasons for this; not enough desire, not enough planning, or not enough motivation. Begin planning your resolution around December 1. Use the tips on goal setting to create a specific and workable plan. If you stick with your resolution you will be able to make one large improvement in your life every year, for the rest of your life.

✦ ✦ ✦

The world is moving so fast these days that the man who says it can't be done is generally interrupted by someone doing it.

Harry Emerson Fosdick

Change Your Thinking Places

If you find yourself becoming mentally unmotivated, switch your surroundings. This could be as simple as changing rooms in your house or office or taking a drive to a nearby location. Try out some of these places:

◇ park
◇ library
◇ friend's house
◇ coffee shop

Picture Perfect (Visualization I)

Visualize the desired outcome in your head. This method is proven to increase motivation and the probability of the event actually occurring. The process of visualization creates new connections in your mind, making the actual activity easier to complete. Find a comfortable place that is free from distraction. Sit down in a comfortable chair and breath deeply. Once you are relaxed, picture yourself accomplishing your goal or dream in your mind. See and feel yourself succeeding, and you'll be motivated to make it a reality.

✦ ✦ ✦

Giving the Common Technique a Twist (Visualization II)

Picture the past in your mind, and realize how far you have come since then. If you have stopped smoking for three months, think back to your smoking days. You'll be glad that you changed your ways and won't want to go back. This technique will keep you heading in the right direction.

✦ ✦ ✦

Make Your Picture Detailed (Visualization III)

When you use visualization to get motivated, make the scene as detailed as possible. If you are picturing your golf game, smell the grass and crisp air. Hear the birds, the wind, and your friends talking. Feel the club in your hand, see the flag waving in the air, and swing away.

✦ ✦ ✦

Write It Down (Visualization IV)

After you see the picture in your mind, write down a description. This is bringing two useful techniques together. The description you write down will be a reminder of where you are heading if you stay on the path.

✦ ✦ ✦

Mix It Up (Visualization V)

Use the visualization techniques with different areas of your life. It may take some creativity, but that will make it more fun. Use the tips with health, wealth, relationships, career, personal success, and happiness. The technique is quick, easy, and it works with everything.

✦ ✦ ✦

Copy What You See (Visualization VI)

Put yourself in the shoes of those whom you admire in movies or stories. If you watch a movie about a woman overcoming all obstacles, picture yourself in her place. This type of visualization is extremely motivating and can be used with movies, stories you read, stories you hear, or even stories that you make up.

✦ ✦ ✦

Choose a Quiet Place (Visualization VII)

Choose a quiet place when you visualize. This technique depends on a concentrated mental effort. Distractions will make the process very difficult. Try your bedroom, den, or front porch for quiet areas. Let the other people in

If one advances confidently in the direction of his dreams, and endeavors to live the life which he has imagined, he will meet with a success unexpected in common hours.

Henry David Thoreau

Vacation

Take a vacation. Getting away from it all for a brief time can work wonders for your attitude and motivation. Put your concerns on hold and enjoy yourself. Possible vacation ideas include:
- ❖ weekend camping trip
- ❖ a week at your relatives
- ❖ a day at the beach

your family know in advance that you will need a little quiet time.

✦ ✦ ✦

Stick with Your Quiet Place (Visualization VIII)

Use the same place each time you visualize. Your body will begin to anticipate the situation and become relaxed quickly. If you constantly change the environment you use, your body will have to readjust each time. When you find a good place that works for you, stick with it.

✦ ✦ ✦

Visualize Often (Visualization IX)

Use the process of visualization often. It is a quick and easy guarantee to motivation. Getting motivated doesn't mean you have to do something new and different every time. Visualization is an effective method to becoming enthusiastic and excited about the possibilities and opportunities in life.

✦ ✦ ✦

The Big Picture (Visualization X)

Dream big. Because it's your picture, you can make it as large or as small as you like. Don't be afraid to think big when visualizing. Stretching beyond your current circumstances is what improvement is all about. Have fun with it and dream big.

✦ ✦ ✦

Analyze the Picture (Visualization XI)

A picture is only worth a thousand words if you take the time to analyze and interpret it. When you create a picture in your mind, think

about what steps you will need to take in order to make the picture come true. Break the picture down into workable goals. You can then create a plan of action and get started on making it happen.

✦ ✦ ✦

Tell the Story to Others (Visualization XII)

Share your picture, if you feel comfortable doing so, with friends and family. The more you talk about it, the more it becomes a part of your everyday life. Once that happens, you will be amazed at how fast you progress.

✦ ✦ ✦

Talk the Talk

If you want to be motivated, speak as if you already are. The words you use in daily conversation play an important role in your attitude and actions. Use phrases like, "I'm motivated to get things done," or "I'll reach my goals." This is a simple way to make a positive change in your life. Try to avoid phrases and words that indicate a lack of motivation and energy.

✦ ✦ ✦

How Do You Look?

How you look says a lot about how you feel. If you want to be successful, motivated, and happy then you must look the part. Hold your head high, walk with confidence, and dress in a manner that properly represents how you wish to be seen. Your looks are part of a circular pattern. The way you look affects how people treat you, which in turn affects your attitude about yourself and life in general.

You see things; and you say "Why?" But I dream things that never were; and I say "Why not?"

George Bernard Shaw

The Greatest Reward of All

Use growth as a motivator. In your career, financially, mentally, physically, and emotionally. Growing as a person and in all areas of your life is the real motivation behind everything you do. Remember, growing into a better person is its own reward. The money, positions, and smaller rewards help, but when it comes down to it, growth is the key.

✧ work promotions
✧ education
✧ personal improvements

You Are What You Think

This is one of the most important lessons you will learn about motivation. If you learn nothing else from this book, walk away with an appreciation for this idea. An example will help to demonstrate the point. Imagine that you want to write a book. Before you chose this goal, you rarely heard anything mentioned about the topic. The next day, after you have decided to write a book, it's on your mind constantly. You notice an ad on television for writers, your ears perk up when an author is on the radio, and when your friend talks about writing a book, you become interested immediately.

You see, when you think of something you begin to see the world in a different light. Before I became involved in motivation, I rarely heard the word. Now that I have dedicated years to the topic, I see, hear, read, and think of the word hundreds of times a day. It is all because of what I chose to think about. Remember, it works the other way as well. If you choose to think negatively, you will see examples all around you that reinforce your negative and damaging thoughts. You are what you think, so think the right things.

✦ ✦ ✦

Positive Self-Talk

Use positive self-talk. When you think about the things you want to accomplish, you will have an easier time making them come true if you use positive thoughts and phrases instead of negative ones. Examples of effective self-talk are, "I can do this," "I won't give up," or "If it has been done before, I can do it again."

The Greatest Thinking Time in the World

At night, as you are getting ready for bed, think. The room is quiet, your body is relaxed, and your mind is free to roam. Input the challenge, and your mind will find a solution. You may realize a new way to tackle a challenge, or think of an idea to help you with your current goal. The power of your mind doesn't stop there, it continues while you dream. Your brain works all night long on the things you feed it. When you wake up in the morning you may just have the answer you've been looking for.

We will either find a way, or make one.

Hannibal

✦ ✦ ✦

You Only Live Once

One of the greatest motivating forces in life is the shortness of life. Human beings live as if their days will never end. If you are afraid to take risks, go after your dreams, accept challenges, or change your life for the better, just do it! Tomorrow, as you have been told many times, may not come. Today is the only time you are guaranteed a chance to improve your life.

✦ ✦ ✦

No Regrets

Live your life in a manner that leaves you with no regrets in the end. If you want to take a risk, but aren't sure what to do, ask yourself if you'll regret the decision later. The saddest thing to hear about is someone who regrets the things they never did. There will come a time when you can't try and try again.

✦ ✦ ✦

Collect Pictures

Use pictures as motivation. When you see a picture of Europe, and you are a hopeful traveler, cut it out and pin it up. If you are trying to get in shape, cut out pictures of a fit body, or if you are trying to stop smoking cut out a picture from a magazine of an unhealthy lung. Cut out the following:

❖ places you want to travel
❖ sites you want to see
❖ things you want to attain
❖ representations of your goals

Great Things Lie Ahead

Besides the 'seize the day' ideas to get motivated, think about what has been accomplished and what could be accomplished if you set your mind to doing something. People have built empires on pure ambition and belief, men and women have single-handedly changed the course of history. Who knows what heights you could reach if you focused your time and energy on one aim. The only way you'll ever know is if you go out there and get to work!

❖ ❖ ❖

Manipulation vs. Motivation

Motivation is healthy, positive, and necessary in every area of your life. Manipulation is damaging, negative, and never necessary. Be careful not to confuse the two. Whether you are helping others to get motivated or are trying to motivate yourself, beware of creating situations resulting in guilt or anger.

❖ ❖ ❖

Three Meals a Day Guarantees the Motivation will Stay

Eat a well-balanced meal. It is a well-known fact that eating the right amounts of food is vital to good health and high energy. Breakfast is the most important meal of the day. It is in the early hours that your body requires nutrients to help get it going. Lunch and dinner keep your dietary needs satisfied. If you find that you are sluggish or tired, ask yourself, "Have I eaten today?"

❖ ❖ ❖

Get Enough Sleep

Sleep at least six to eight hours per night. I can't believe my ears when I hear people tell me that they get by on three to four hours of sleep a night. It's not healthy and is doing more damage to their system than they realize. Six to eight hours is necessary for the adult body to recuperate from the day's activities. Don't let sleep be the thing you sacrifice for the sake of others. After enough sacrificing of sleep, you won't be able to take part in any activities.

I am always doing things I can't do, that's how I get to do them.

Pablo Picasso

♦ ♦ ♦

The 15 Minute Cat Nap

Take a fifteen minute break each day to rest and relax. To give your body a break, lie on the floor for fifteen minutes. The firm surface is great for the body. A quick fifteen minute break can help you maintain energy and motivation throughout the remainder of the day.

♦ ♦ ♦

Exercise

Exercise daily. This can include many activities and isn't limited to simply running. You can do aerobics, jog, swim, lift weights, play sports, or chase your kids around the house. Exercising will give you more energy, strength, motivation, and improved health. Create a complete plan and stick with it.

♦ ♦ ♦

Get a Check-Up

To start things off right with your health plan, get a check-up from you doctor. As with all

Pick a Symbol

Choose an object that symbolizes what you want to achieve, be, or do. Keep the object close to you wherever you go. This small charm comes in handy because it represents the words, feelings, and thoughts you have about your goal all in one compact object. Try these ideas out for your own symbol of motivation:

- ◇ picture
- ◇ photograph
- ◇ key chain
- ◇ charm
- ◇ coin
- ◇ quotation

programs, processes, and systems for improvement, you must first take inventory of where you are now before you think about where you want to go.

✦ ✦ ✦

Take a Walk

Take a walk around the block to clear your mind and think. The process of thinking is actually what gets you motivated. If you are planning a trip to Europe, while walking you can think about the places you are going to see, and the people you are going to meet. This will get you excited and motivated about making it happen.

✦ ✦ ✦

Take a Drive

If the weather doesn't permit a walk, take a drive instead. Getting away from your work or problems will help you to gain a new perspective on the situation. Taking a step back to see things from a different viewpoint will allow you to see new solutions to old obstacles.

✦ ✦ ✦

Take a Bike Ride

Take an hour bike ride on the weekend. You'll be able to hit two birds with one stone as you exercise and give yourself some time to think. There is nothing better than making progress in two areas with only one activity.

✦ ✦ ✦

De-stress

Take specific actions to decrease your stress levels. A main deterrent to changing your

present circumstances to enhance motivation is stress. Stress can cause great harm to your system and shouldn't be dealt with lightly. If you want to be truly motivated and focused on your goals, you must first de-stress. You will find many tips on reducing stress and tension in later chapters.

✦ ✦ ✦

The Only Way to Succeed

There is only one way to improve your life. There is only one way to succeed. There is only one way to make positive changes in your life. The answer is work. You have to be willing to get out there and put in the time and effort. You have to be willing to face failures and carry on. Less than 1% of success results from luck or chance alone. If you are ready to work hard, there is little that you cannot achieve.

✦ ✦ ✦

The Gift

Accomplishments that are given to you will not be satisfying. Imagine that you want to be a star athlete in the NBA. With a snap of my fingers, you have the talent, and have already won several championships. You do not, however, have any recollection of gaining those talents, of training, or of improving your skills. You were simply given the ability. Would you feel satisfied? Maybe, at first, but after time you wouldn't value your talents because you didn't work for them, you didn't really accomplish anything. The moral is that you have to put in hard work and effort in order for you to feel satisfied and successful when you reach your goals.

Destiny is not a matter of chance, it is a matter of choice; it is not a thing to be waited for, it is a thing to be achieved.

William Jennings Bryan

Quotations

Look for, save, and remember inspiring quotations. If you find one especially useful, jot it down and keep it handy. In times of need, you'll have a small but important tool to help you get moving. You can find great quotations:

- ❖ in books
- ❖ online
- ❖ from friends
- ❖ on television
- ❖ in magazines

The Real Success Stories

You've heard about those success stories. One day a man has an innovative idea and the next day he's a millionaire. This perception of success and fortune is very misleading. What you hear about is the glamorous lifestyle, the wealth, and success. What you don't often hear about is how hard that man or woman worked, and how many sacrifices they made to get where they are today. Remember that the success stories you hear have hard work, dedication, and perseverance at their core.

❖ ❖ ❖

Free Day

Give yourself a free day to rest and relax. If possible, use a weekend so you won't have to miss any work. The hard part isn't in taking a break, but in letting go of stress and worry as you do so. When you take a break from work and worry, don't let problems creep into the equation.

❖ ❖ ❖

Your Notepad

Carry a small notepad with you wherever you go. Great ideas and thoughts jump in and out of your mind every minute. To make the best of these revelations jot them down in a small notebook. At the end of the day, page through your notebook to elaborate on ideas, or eliminate some altogether. You never know what you'll be able to come up with when those key thoughts are captured on paper.

❖ ❖ ❖

The Night Stand Notepad

Keep a notepad and pen on your night stand. The ideas that come to you in the night while you are sleeping are some of the best ideas you'll ever think of. Your mind has had hours to mull over your past, present and future, which brings several key ideas to you without you even knowing it! When you wake in the middle of the night with a great idea, jot it down in your night stand notebook. You'll be able to catch those ideas that before would have been lost.

✦ ✦ ✦

Television Time

Keep a pen and paper on the coffee table or end table to record the thoughts that jump into your head while watching your television. The shows and programs you watch at night contain stories, thoughts, ideas, theories, statistics, opinions, excitement, tips, techniques, answers and questions. Your mind is inundated with visual stimuli that make your brain work overtime. This is when you need to write down the things that you want to remember for the future.

✦ ✦ ✦

Tape Recorder to the Rescue

Use a hand-held tape recorder to save ideas and thoughts that come to you. This tool is especially handy in situations where you can't easily write things down. For example, if you have a great idea while driving in the car you can just push record while waiting at a stoplight and talk away. At the end of the day you'll have tons of great ideas to work with.

Keep sowing your seed, for you never know which will grow-perhaps it all will.

Ecclesiastes

Create a Personal Mantra

Create a phrase that puts you at ease or gets you motivated. *Life is short, Don't sweat the small stuff*, or *I can do this* are good examples of personal sayings to put you in a motivated frame of mind.

From Tape to Paper

Write out the things you tape on your recorder. Dealing with the written word is much easier than a tape recorded message. When it's written down, you can adjust, reformat, and edit your ideas.

✦ ✦ ✦

Categorize Your Lists

Once you have collected all of your items from your notepads, notebooks, and tape recorder, it's time to bring some order to the heap of information. Create several categories that represent major areas of your life. Health, wealth, success, and happiness are the four pillars with which I categorize my work. Any topics that you choose will work fine. Place each of your items into one of the categories.

✦ ✦ ✦

Prioritize Your Lists

After each item is in its category, prioritize the items. Begin with the top item first, and work your way down the list as you accomplish the tasks. Prioritizing will ensure that the most important items are accomplished first.

✦ ✦ ✦

Public Speakers

Go listen to a public speaker. The public speaking industry is growing rapidly and offers speakers on every topic imaginable. Programs on personal happiness and success, business, starting a new career, improving your health, growing your wealth and much more are offered by thousands of public

speakers all over the country. Look online or in the newspaper for information on speakers in your area.

✦ ✦ ✦

Audiotapes

Listen to audio program. Regardless of what needs you have, there are audio programs that cover your topic. The benefits of audiotapes include hands-free learning, finding particular information quickly, and being able to listen in many different places.

✦ ✦ ✦

Video Programs

Purchase video programs for education and motivation. You can also check out programs from your local library. Searching for video-cassette programs on the Internet will return thousands upon thousands of results. Watching a video is a great way to obtain information in an easy-to-learn format.

✦ ✦ ✦

Create a Motivational CD

Put together a CD containing your favorite songs. You can even purchase CD's that already contain motivating music. When you wake up, work out, or need to relax you'll have music to get things going.

✦ ✦ ✦

Books, Books, and more Books

Read books. Motivation is created from knowledge. For instance, when you know the steps involved in playing the guitar, you will become more motivated to learn how to do it. When you know how a man lost thirty

The answer is simple; if you want something very badly, you can achieve it.

Margo Jones

The Wish List

Make a list of ten dreams that you have. It doesn't matter how big they are. Keep the list in a desk drawer. Take the list out to daydream, alleviate stress, or for motivation.

pounds you will become excited about doing the same. Books are one of the greatest mediums for gaining knowledge. Aside from how-to books, there are books that inspire, excite, motivate, and calm.

✦ ✦ ✦

Internet

Many times throughout this book you have seen mention of the vast and powerful Internet, and here it is again. The Internet brings the world to you with a mouse click. It doesn't matter what you need, you'll find valuable and relevant information on the net.

✦ ✦ ✦

Poems

Read poetry to become inspired. A key focus of many poets is to use words to motivate others to action. With this in mind, the poets of our time, and those that came before them, offer their unique patterns of words to help you see the world differently.

✦ ✦ ✦

Motivational Programs

Need to get motivated? Then take part in a motivational program. Motivational speakers make up a large niche of the speaking market. Thousands of programs have been created whose sole aim is to motivate people.

✦ ✦ ✦

Magazines

Subscribe to magazines that offer tips and ideas in the areas that interest you. Many of today's magazines are made up of excellent articles and features that are geared towards

helping readers improve their lives with simple tips and ideas. Pick one up today and see what you can learn.

✦ ✦ ✦

Newsletters

Magazines aren't the only forms of information that offer a great deal of value to its readers. Newsletters, both off-line and online, are a must for the motivated mind. Stay on top of your interests with the use of newsletters.

✦ ✦ ✦

Calculators

Keep a calculator close for number crunching. This can serve as a very effective motivator. A calculator allows you to create very specific numerical goals, along with breaking those goals down into sub-goals.

✦ ✦ ✦

Meeting People

Meet at least one new person each month. Neighbors, friends of friends, or coworkers you haven't met yet are good places to start. Your happiness is made up of several parts, the majority being the relationships you have with others. This is a great way to expand the number of great friendships you have.

Only those who do nothing make no mistakes.

Anonymous

2

Outsourcing Motivation

YOU CAN GET MOTIVATED and enjoy accomplishments alone, but sharing it with others not only makes the successes much sweeter, it also makes getting motivated a much easier task. This section is all about getting motivated through the help of other people. You'll find that many of the tips will not only motivate you but also the other person involved.

Two brains, as they say, are better than one, and that is definitely true when it comes to motivation. If you have been having trouble getting started by yourself, the following tips will help you solve that motivational challenge.

Seek Out the Experts

Find the experts in your particular area of interest. Be a sponge and soak in every ounce of information and inspiration you can. They have been through the troubles you will meet. They have overcome the challenges you are now facing. Seek out the people who have already done what you want to do. After finding the contact information you can:

- send an e-mail
- write a letter
- call them on the phone
- send them a fax

Giving-Up Goals

Tell your friends about your giving-up goals. These are things that you no longer wish to do, you are giving something up. Smoking, over-eating, procrastinating and swearing are examples of giving-up goals. These types of goals are great to share with everyone. Your friends and family won't let you get away with breaking your word very often, so share these types of goals with them as much as you can.

✦ ✦ ✦

Going-Up

Tell close friends and family members about your going-up goal. Getting a promotion is a going-up goal When you share these goals with co-workers and friends, it may come off as bragging or being competitive. When you share these goals with close family members you will receive the support and motivation you require.

✦ ✦ ✦

Progress Report

Have your friends and family check in on your progress. Tell them that you welcome feedback and reminders. You may become too busy to stay on top of your goals, but those around you won't easily forget. Having someone to ask you about your goals will help to keep you reminded of what you set out to do.

✦ ✦ ✦

Group Goals

Create team goals if you work at a place where the objectives are team oriented. You can also set group goals in the home. Use the systems contained in this book to help you put together an effective strategy. When others are involved in the process, you will be responsible for the results. This always helps to motivate people, and it will do the same for you.

✦ ✦ ✦

Mail, Fax, E-mail, Call

Communicate your goals to others any way you can. Send an e-mail to your friends describing your current goal. Call your relatives and talk about what you plan on doing. You could even write a letter to a friend about your future plans. As you begin to share your goals with other people it will start to take on a life of its own. It will grow and develop into something that you cannot forget.

✦ ✦ ✦

Communicate Importance

In order for the process of sharing to help motivate you, the ones you tell must first understand the importance of the situation. Explain to them that you are sincere about your goal and that their help is greatly appreciated.

✦ ✦ ✦

How Do They Do It?

Ask the people in your life what steps they take to get motivated. Each individual has their own way of getting excited about something. Unless you ask them, you'll never know what secrets they keep. After learning about their tips, you can offer some of your own.

✦ ✦ ✦

Converse, converse, converse, with living men, face to face, mind to mind—that is one of the best sources of knowledge.

Daniel Webster

The Buddy Meeting

Create a weekly or monthly meeting for you and your buddy. At the meeting include ideas that increased your motivation and things that decreased it. In time you will have hundreds of ideas to help you get motivated for every activity and job that comes your way. To make each meeting more effective, consider the following tips:

✧ keep notes during the meeting
✧ tape record your sessions
✧ have a plan before you begin

A Student of Motivation

Observe others in person or on the television to see how they get motivated. This doesn't allow you to speak with the person, but it is just as useful.

✦ ✦ ✦

Use a Questionnaire at Work

Distribute a productivity questionnaire at work. Include questions regarding motivation, focus, and energy. Distribute your questionnaire to employees above and below you. Lower-level positions may have very different answers from those in high-level positions.

✦ ✦ ✦

Your Personal Motivator

Find a friend who is willing to help you with your goals and motivation. Having someone help you is priceless. They will be able to offer advice, support, motivation, suggestions, and a listening ear. You don't have to go at this alone.

✦ ✦ ✦

Buddy Up

Find a friend who would like to create a motivation buddy system. You motivate her, and she motivates you. You share your successes or failures with her, and she does the same. You can also teach her about tips that worked well for you. The buddy system uses two brains for one goal, motivation.

✦ ✦ ✦

The Big Buddy

If you find that the buddy system works well, create a larger network of people to take part in the process. Find three to five people who would like to be a little more motivated in their lives. This is a powerful way to make your life better.

✦ ✦ ✦

The Reason Behind the Naysayer (Negative Reactions I)

You will come across them more times than you would like to in your lifetime. People who think you are crazy for trying to do what you want to do. People who are certain that you will fail in your endeavors. People who aren't willing to take the steps you are taking, and in turn offer nothing but negative reactions. If I see you take risks that I am not willing to take, and you succeed, I may not respond positively because of jealousy and resentment. Naysayers come about more because of their limits and fears, not yours. Realize that you can do anything you set your mind to, regardless of what the naysayers may think.

✦ ✦ ✦

What Do They Say? (Negative Reactions II)

When you hear someone saying you can't do this or that, listen for the reasons in their words. Use their reasons as your strong points. For instance, if someone says, after hearing that you are trying to quit smoking, "You'll never do it. You smoke every night," use 'not smoking at night' as one of your sub-goals.

✦ ✦ ✦

I not only use all the brains I have but all that I can borrow.

Thomas Woodrow
Wilson

The Agenda

Here is a possible agenda for your network meetings:

- ✧ exchange contact information
- ✧ have each individual write down a goal
- ✧ exchange personal experiences regarding goals
- ✧ create specific plans for each goal
- ✧ set a time for the next meeting
- ✧ during the week, contact your buddies about progress
- ✧ at the next meeting, share your progress and problems
- ✧ brainstorm solutions
- ✧ when a goal is accomplished, start the process over

Prove Them Wrong (Negative Reactions III)

We don't want you dancing around chanting victory songs in your friends' faces, but internally you can benefit from the naysayer's words. Use them as motivation. Time and again I hear successful businessmen and women, athletes, authors, and hundreds of other people who have reached great heights state that they are where they are today because someone, somewhere, said they couldn't do it.

✦ ✦ ✦

Make Verbal Commitments

Keeping your word to others is important. Because of this, verbal commitments to your goals are a great way to increase your motivation. If you know that other people are aware of your dedication, you won't be easily sidetracked from your initial course.

✦ ✦ ✦

Make a Written Commitment

To go one step further, write out your commitment and offer it to someone whom you trust and respect. If you have a habit of keeping your word this will work, guaranteed. If you have trouble keeping your word, this will help you improve in that area of your life.

3

Breaking Habits

B AD HABITS ARE HARD TO DROP and even harder to
live with. When the correct steps are taken, a bad
habit can be stopped dead in its tracks. It doesn't matter what habits you have, you can change. You can take
the bad and replace it with good.

The next section offers tips that help you to drop bad
habits and pick up new ones. By putting these ideas to
work for you today, you will eventually break free of
unhealthy and negative tendencies and replace them
with healthy, positive activities.

Habit Specifics

Clearly state your habit. Make a written or mental list of the specific things that make up your negative tendencies. Include the following in your list:

✧ when you do it
✧ when you started it
✧ how you do it
✧ where you do it

Three Weeks to Completion

When you feel like you'll never be able to drop your bad habit, remember this; it takes approximately three weeks to break an old habit. That means you cannot expect instant results and immediate success. You have to be willing to put in the time. Knowing that it takes three weeks should help you to maintain your motivation and positive attitude throughout the process. Be patient.

✦ ✦ ✦

Temptation

Take steps to eliminate habit temptation from your life. If you are trying to lose weight, eliminate fatty foods from your groceries. If you are trying to stop smoking, make sure your home is free of cigarettes. Simply eliminating the temptation from your daily life will go a long way to helping you break the habit.

✦ ✦ ✦

A Great Resource

Write out the reasons why you want to break your bad habit. This list will serve as motivation whenever you need it. When you are feeling weak, you can take a look at your list and remember why you started the process in the first place.

✦ ✦ ✦

Just the Facts

Get the information about your bad habit. One tool they use to warn children about the dangers of smoking is a picture of a smoker's lung. The more you can learn about the nega-

tive side of your habit, the easier it will be for you to say no. They say that knowledge is power, and that sentiment holds true here. As your knowledge and education increases, so too will your motivation to break the habit.

✦ ✦ ✦

The Reverse Reward

After talking with individuals who are trying to give up a bad habit, I have come across a common obstacle that I like to call the Reverse Reward. They reward themselves with the very thing they were trying to give up. For example, someone who is trying to eat healthier, after doing so for a week, eats junk food as a reward. This is crazy thinking, and it happens all the time! Do not reward your improvement with the bad habit you are trying to give up.

✦ ✦ ✦

The Smart Reward

Reward yourself with something that contributes to your plan. This may take some creativity, but with enough thought you can come up with quite a few ideas. If you are trying to get in shape, reward yourself with a healthy meal. The right reward system will get you motivated and help you reach your goals.

✦ ✦ ✦

How To Make It Happen

If you are giving something up, pick a new habit to replace the old. When you have something better to replace your bad habit with, you will be able to fend off temptations. Great examples of habit replacement are working

We are what we repeatedly do. Excellence then, is not an act, but a habit.

Aristotle

The Reason Behind Your Habit

Look to the source of your habit. What do you get from it that you enjoy or need? Once you understand why you want it, you can find a smart replacement or solution to the problem. Putting your energy towards the symptoms of the problem will get you nowhere. You have to go to the source of it all.

out instead of smoking, running in the morning instead of oversleeping, and helping others instead of having a negative attitude.

◆ ◆ ◆

Peer Pressure

Picture yourself trying to improve your attitude while spending time with some of the most negative people you know. It sounds like quite a losing battle, and it is. It may seem obvious reading these lines, but it happens all the time. It is very hard to give up a bad habit, and the difficulty doubles when those around you offer no support or understanding. You don't have to stop spending time with your friends. You simply have to be aware that these situations create obstacles between you and your goal.

◆ ◆ ◆

The Best Company

Spend time with others who are also trying to give up a bad habit. You will be able to motivate, support, and help each other as you strive to make your lives better. You could also involve yourself with those who have already conquered their bad habits. They will be able to offer you knowledge and experience that will come in handy in the future.

◆ ◆ ◆

Write a Mission Statement

Write out, in one sentence, your own personal mission statement. This will help to keep you heading in the right direction when you feel like giving up. Keep it simple and to the point.

◆ ◆ ◆

Tell the World

The more people you tell about your goal, the more supporters you'll have. Tell your friends, family, co-workers, neighbors, and anyone else who will listen that you are trying to give up your bad habit. Doing this will make you accountable to many other people, and they will no doubt help you stick to your commitment.

✦ ✦ ✦

The Start

A great plan is useless until you put it into action. That is why you need a start date. After making a written commitment to change, write down the day you will begin your plan. Make this date reasonable and challenging. Putting off the start until next year is too far away, but starting in five minutes may also be ineffective.

✦ ✦ ✦

Picture In Your Mind

Create an image in your mind of the person you are hoping to become. See yourself eliminating your habit and beginning a new, positive activity. If you can visualize and see the new and improved you, you'll find instant motivation for making your picture a reality.

✦ ✦ ✦

Pictures are Worth 1,001 Words

Place a picture of someone you admire or look up to in your home or office. You can also put their picture in your wallet or purse. This will act as a small reminder and motivation to stick with your plan. If you are trying to

A man who gives his children habits of industry provides for them better than by giving them a fortune.

Richard Whately

The Getaway

When you feel like giving in, do something completely different immediately. This will get your mind off of your habit and put your energies somewhere positive. Many people have had success with breaking away with the following activities:

- ✧ working out
- ✧ cleaning
- ✧ running
- ✧ playing sports
- ✧ hobbies

drop your negativity, you could place a picture of your children in your wallet. When someone frustrates you, simply take out their picture and let their smiles become yours.

✦ ✦ ✦

Join a Support Group

Depending on what you are trying to give up, there are many support groups that offer information and resources that can help you with your progress. Learning from those who are in the same boat, or from others who have succeeded, can prove to be a priceless experience. There is no better way to learn and educate yourself about the facts and solutions than joining forces with other people in similar circumstances.

✦ ✦ ✦

Start Your Own Group

If you know of several other people that are trying to break the same bad habits, create your own group. A group of individuals doesn't have to meet in a certified institution to offer help and support. Simply sharing your experiences, ideas, and successes with others is a great way to maintain motivation and confidence in your ability to make it.

✦ ✦ ✦

Get Professional Help

If nothing else seems to be working, you may need to seek professional help. Dietitians, psychiatrists, psychologists, doctors, and professional organizations and groups have helped thousands of people rid themselves of self-defeating behaviors.

✦ ✦ ✦

Contract

Using a word processing program, type out a contract to yourself. Within this document you can state your goal, the start date, and your deadline. Sign and date the contract, and place it in a frame on your wall. Every day you see that piece of paper you will be reminded of the promise you made to yourself.

✦ ✦ ✦

Before and After Motivation

If applicable, take before and after pictures. For example, if you are trying to lose weight, take a photograph before you start exercising and eating healthier. After several weeks take another photograph and compare the results. Change may come slowly, but it will come nonetheless. Use these pictorial representations of success to keep your energy and dedication to the goal at the highest levels possible.

✦ ✦ ✦

It's Not Just You

Make a list of other people who are affected by your negative habit. Take smoking, for example; the statistics on secondhand smoke are chilling and proven to be accurate. This negative habit not only hurts you, but also the ones that are closest to you. Remember this when you are thinking about giving up.

✦ ✦ ✦

The Success Story

A major part of the organizations that help people to quit is the sharing of success stories. When you can listen to someone share

We first make our habits, and then our habits make us.

John Dryden

Track Your Progress

An important factor in staying motivated is knowing that you are progressing. As you work to eliminate negative habits from your life, track your progress. If you are trying to quit smoking, keep track of how many cigarettes you smoke a day. Work to decrease that number over time. It is much easier to stay motivated when you see small, constant improvements than to focus only on the end results.

their story of struggle and ultimate success, you feel like you can make it too. You can relate to those who have been in your shoes, and that is why you must create a collection of your own success stories. When you read a story in a magazine, cut it out and place it in a motivational story file. When you hear a story from a friend, write or type it out and save it for the future. The more success stories you can get your hands on, the more motivation you will have to join their ranks.

4

Beating Procrastination

PROCRASTINATION IS MOTIVATION'S WORST ENEMY. It says, "wait until tomorrow," and puts its victim into a drowsy and dreary sleep of inaction. Don't give up just yet, there is hope. Procrastination might have control over you now, but after using the following tips you'll be free and clear of this quicksand-like trap.

The following section includes tips and techniques that will help you kick the procrastination habit and do what needs to be done. With proven systems and ideas you'll be motivated in no time at all.

Delegate

If you dread doing something, see if you can have someone else do it. Putting your responsibilities on someone else's shoulders isn't the best solution, but you may just find that there is someone you know who actually enjoys the task.

The Hardest Thing To Do

Just start! It's like you are at the top of a large mountain and the first step will be enough to get you rolling. Taking that first step, if only a small one, is usually enough to get you going. Plan on doing the activity that you are avoiding for only a few minutes. You may find that the time flies by and you are at the end before you know it.

✦ ✦ ✦

Do the Worst First

Put the things you like least in the beginning of the process and you'll have the motivation to reach the good stuff at the end. If you dislike studying calculus but love learning about history, leave the history for the end. If you would rather skip the weights but look forward to the aerobics, lift weights first. Saving the enjoyable activities for the end will help you to get through the beginning.

✦ ✦ ✦

The Right Reasons

Ask yourself why you think you need to do whatever it is that you are avoiding. State the reasons why you want to or have to do it. Each reason you include in your list will be motivation. If you cannot clearly say why you want or need to do it, perhaps you shouldn't be doing it at all.

✦ ✦ ✦

The Means to the End

Think of the ultimate goal when you are having trouble starting. This works well when you have to do something you don't want to do in order to come closer to your overall goal. For example, if you want to buy a car you have to forgo some spending. You may not want to save money, but thinking about the ultimate goal will help keep you motivated.

✦ ✦ ✦

Small Steps

You don't have to tackle the entire goal, chore, activity, job, task, project, or assignment all at once. You can take small steps, and as long as they are in the right direction, you'll complete the journey. Constantly remind yourself that it takes many small steps to create an enormous success. You can take small steps, regardless of what the activity is.

✦ ✦ ✦

The Longer You Wait . . .

Don't wait too long to start. The longer you wait, the less time you have to get going, the less energy you'll have to do a thorough job, and the less motivation you'll have to finish. Procrastination makes things more difficult to accomplish. If you know you should do it, have the tools to do it, and have the time to get started, then just do it.

✦ ✦ ✦

Motivation & Index Cards

Write out on an index card the thing you are avoiding. Place the card or cards in areas that you pass by often. You can put them on the fridge, on the bathroom mirror, in your purse or wallet, or on your desk. These small reminders will help to get you motivated to start working.

✦ ✦ ✦

Putting off an easy thing makes it hard, and putting off a hard thing makes it impossible.

George Lorimer

Dirty Dishes

When is a dirty dish easiest to clean? Immediately. The same is true of the tasks and chores you are putting off. As you wait longer the dish becomes harder to clean and more of a nuisance than before. Do what you have to do now before you end up with too many dirty dishes that won't come clean.

Just Say It

Say the thing that you are putting off. "I am going to start writing my novel," or "I will go running today." These simple statements cause your brain to concentrate more on the doing and less on the procrastination. Don't merely say it in your head, say it out loud and to anyone who will listen.

✦ ✦ ✦

Concentrate on What is in Front of You

Focus on the task at hand and not what follows next. This can cause a decrease in motivation. If you are cleaning the kitchen but think only of the trouble that will come when you reach the basement, your motivation will decrease. You would be letting future steps impede on your current tasks. Keep your attention on what you are doing now, and wait until the next step before you put thought into it.

✦ ✦ ✦

Timing is Everything

Set aside a day and time that you will start and finish chores and tasks that you don't like doing. For example, every Sunday for two hours you and your family could clean the house. When the time comes, whether you want to or not, you just do it.

✦ ✦ ✦

When It's Finally Over

Close your eyes and picture what it will feel like when you are finally finished. Whether it's homework, working out, eating healthy, giving up smoking, waking up early, being positive, helping others, or writing a book, you will have the motivation you desire after seeing the finished product in your mind. If you simply start now, you will get there.

✦ ✦ ✦

Procrastination Partners

Find a friend to work with who is trying to start doing a similar thing. You will motivate, support, and enjoy success together. Having a partner to work with makes goal achievement and motivation so much easier. Start thinking today about someone who could be your Procrastination Partner.

✦ ✦ ✦

Don't Think Too Much

Just do it. If you think about it too much you might build up more mental resistance than if you just started in the first place. After sitting around and thinking how much you don't want to do something, you are creating an impossible situation for yourself. Decide what needs to be done, and do it.

✦ ✦ ✦

Chores to the Rescue

If your procrastination peaks when it comes to doing chores around the house, a new perspective can make all the difference in the world. Instead of dreading the jobs, focus 100% on what you are doing. This simple change in attention will relieve stress from other responsibilities or worries you may have. When you are completely wrapped up in one job it will be hard to think about everything else that is on your list. If you are

Know the true value of time; snatch, seize, and enjoy every moment of it. No idleness; no laziness; no procrastination; never put off till tomorrow what you can do today.

Lord Chesterfield

What's Up?

What's making you procrastinate? What are you avoiding? If you can't seem to start working on a goal you have created, perhaps you need to take a second look at what you thought you wanted. Chores and required work are different, you usually just have to do it. It's a different story when you are putting off things you once desired.

cleaning the kitchen, focus on the soap, water, and sponge.

◆ ◆ ◆

Make It a Personal Challenge

For some, a challenge is the greatest motivator of all. If you aren't looking forward to doing something, make it a personal goal to do it the best you can. If you are studying for a test, challenge yourself to get an 'A'. This will help to get you from the thinking stage to the doing stage.

◆ ◆ ◆

15 Minute Rule

The dreaded chore: cleaning the kitchen, organizing the closet, or doing the bills. If you have a chore or job that you don't especially look forward to, give it only 15 minutes of your time. Telling yourself this before you start makes getting started a lot easier. Who knows, you may even start to enjoy the chore after all.

◆ ◆ ◆

Swap Responsibilities

Find someone to swap jobs with. If you hate cleaning and your husband hates to wash dishes, swap chores. It's a quick and easy way to overcome procrastination immediately.

5

Constant Curiosity

EDUCATION AND CURIOSITY are vital to motivation. The desire to learn something new goes hand in hand with success, enthusiasm, and ultimate accomplishment. The more you know about your goal, the easier it will be to stay motivated.

The next group of ideas is about simple ways you can learn more about the things you are trying to accomplish, or simply learn more about the world around you. Your brain is like any other muscle in the body, it needs to be worked out. Give it a workout and start giving it some new information to work out with. In the end you'll be smarter, happier, and most importantly, motivated.

Visiting Seminars

Look for upcoming seminars that interest you. A seminar provides more than a book or magazine can because it is interactive. You can ask questions, delve deeper in the particular topics, and even speak personally with the seminar leader. Look to these resources for upcoming seminars:

- library newsletters or bulletins
- newspapers
- local Community Center
- internet
- friends and family

Never Leave Home Without One

Bring a book with you wherever you go. Put one in the car, in your purse, in your briefcase, in your backpack, or in your hand. You never know when you'll get a few moments to yourself, so be prepared and keep a book close.

✦ ✦ ✦

The Greatest Bookmark System in the World

Using a bookmark simply to keep your page is overlooking a much more effective use for that slip of paper. When you read any book, do so with your bookmark and a pen or pencil. As you come across interesting ideas or valuable information, note on the bookmark what page it was on, and where on the page the information was. If it was at the top, put a dash at the top. If it was in the middle, put a dash in the middle and so on. That way, when you go back to the pages you'll know exactly where to find the desired information.

✦ ✦ ✦

Compilation

Once you have completed a book, and you have jotted down notes and page numbers on your bookmark, set aside a time during the week to compile the information. You could type it into a word processing program, or write it out by hand. This system will make each book you read a real value for you. Many people read a book and that's the last they ever think of the contents. You now have a system to really digest what each book contains.

✦ ✦ ✦

Sharing Knowledge

Swap books with your friends and family. You may read some unhelpful books if you just guess at what to choose. When you swap with other people you will be getting a personal recommendation.

✦ ✦ ✦

Once a Month

Read at least one book a month. I have heard many people say that they haven't read a book for years. That is one reason why they have trouble with their motivation. Read non-fiction, fiction, or textbooks. It doesn't always matter what you read. The important part is that you are reading something.

✦ ✦ ✦

Library Day

Set up a library day for your family. Once a week or month, make a trip to the library to check out some new books. Bring your children along and let them choose books they like.

✦ ✦ ✦

Get to Know Your Librarian

It may sound a little strange, but getting to know your librarian will help you find the books and resources you are looking for in half the time. You'll also be updated on new items that come into the library.

✦ ✦ ✦

Keep a Book in the Car

You never know when you'll be stuck in traffic, or worse, stuck because of weather or

Change is the end result of all true learning.

Leo F. Buscaglia

The Phone, Computers, and More!

Discover how things around the house work. Take apart an old phone, read about the invention of the computer, and research how the light bulb lights. Becoming interested in the things in your home will spark your curiosity. Try to find the answers to these questions:

◇ where was the telephone invented?
◇ who built the first television set?
◇ when was the first light bulb invented?
◇ when was the Internet created?

some other uncontrollable factor. In these situations, you can use your time wisely by reading. Keep a book in the glove compartment so you will always have a learning tool nearby when circumstances make one necessary.

✦ ✦ ✦

Switch It Off and Open One Up

At least once a week decide to read instead of watching television. Following this simple process will allow you to read a book per month, and that is just during your normal television time. Coupled with the other book tips you'll be able to read several books a month and increase your knowledge tenfold.

✦ ✦ ✦

Internet Book Stores

Sign up for an account at an online bookstore. The larger businesses offer many features that make finding great books quick and easy. They can tell you what books fit your interests, keep you up to date on new titles, and even send you an e-mail when a new book comes out that is similar to your previous purchases.

✦ ✦ ✦

Join a Book Club

Check into joining a local book club. You will get the opportunity to read interesting material and discuss its meanings, lessons, and values with others. Along with discovering new books, you will be meeting new and interesting people. Two birds with one stone!

✦ ✦ ✦

Become a Member of Your Local Library

If you haven't already, get library cards for you and every member of your family. The library is one of the only organizations that offer such valuable and readily available resources for anyone to use. Become a frequent visitor to your local library. If the library in your town is small, you may want to get a membership at a neighboring one to increase the amount of information you will be able to get your hands on.

The cure for boredom is curiosity. There is no cure for curiosity.

Ellen Parr

✦ ✦ ✦

Create Your Own Book Club

If you aren't interested in joining a book club, create your own. It's simple to do, and also fun for you and your friends. Purchase or check out from the library several copies of the same book. Distribute the books to friends and family who are interested in taking part in your club. Set a general schedule and meet on a regular basis to discuss the book.

✦ ✦ ✦

Reread Your Books

You aren't done learning after you read a book once. There is no way you could decipher all of the intended information after only one reading. It is like a movie. If you watch a movie more than once, you'll notice things that you didn't before. If you found a book interesting or insightful, read it again. I guarantee you will realize things that you didn't see the first time.

✦ ✦ ✦

CD's that Teach

There are many educational programs in the marketplace that are for your desktop computer. This makes maneuverability quick and easy. If you would rather see visual demonstrations and hear explanations instead of reading, this may just be the answer you've been looking for.

The Book Referral System

When you come across a great book, spread the word. Tell your friends, co-workers, and family about what you have found and that you think it would be beneficial to them. In return, ask them to let you know about the books they found informative and interesting.

✦ ✦ ✦

The Library that Travels with You

When you have audiotapes in the car, you've got the perfect traveling library. Instead of listening to radio stations, pop in an audiotape and enjoy the ride. This idea works well for short rides to the office as well as longer road trips.

✦ ✦ ✦

Television Replacement

When you want to sit in front of the set and stare into the screen, listen to an informational audiotape instead. You'll soon find that watching television has become a rare pastime and constant learning has become your passion.

✦ ✦ ✦

Bedtime Stories

For a great bedtime story that teaches, listen to your informational audiotapes while you are falling asleep. This isn't the 'learn a new language while you sleep' idea at work. It is simply another way you can digest information and increase your knowledge and motivation to learn more.

✦ ✦ ✦

Jogging Buddy

You have a few choices when you go jogging. When you will go, for how long, what you will wear, where you will go and most importantly what you will listen to while running. Try listening to your tapes instead of the radio. If replacing music 100% of the time doesn't work for you, listen to tapes half of the run or for half of your jogging days per week.

✦ ✦ ✦

Morning Routine with a Twist

After you have rubbed your eyes and stumbled out of bed, push play on your tape player and take in some insights and thoughts from your audio program. It's a great way to start the day.

✦ ✦ ✦

An Informed Lunch Break

Bring books, tapes, newsletters, or magazines to work. During lunch breaks you will have more than enough material to look through and learn from. This is a simple way to use your free time effectively.

✦ ✦ ✦

Television Guides

Many of the tips are for replacing television with other activities. This doesn't mean that T.V. doesn't have something to offer. Specials on history, science, the future, and more, bring a great deal of information to your home. It's also important to just relax and have fun. Go through your T.V. guide and highlight the specials and programs that you want to view.

✦ ✦ ✦

When the student is ready, the master appears.

Buddhist proverb

Once a Day

Learn something new every day. It doesn't matter how large or how small, just that you increase your knowledge in some way every single day.

Blank Videotape

Keep a blank tape next to the television. Planning ahead will allow you to tape specials and programs that interest you. Normally half of the show is over by the time you finally get your hands on a tape. By the time you get it rolling you realize the tape has one of your favorite movies on it. Skip all of these challenges and keep a few blank tapes next to the television.

✦ ✦ ✦

History Channel, Discovery Channel, and More

Sitcoms, movies, and cartoons are enjoyable, but they shouldn't make up your entire programming needs. Check out programs that offer topics such as history, science, technology or business.

✦ ✦ ✦

Workshops

Take part in a workshop. This is a smaller setting for information dissemination. Usually speaking to a smaller group of 25 or less, a workshop is a hands-on experience where an expert offers his or her support, guidance, and experience in their particular area of interest. Some of the most popular workshops include writing workshops, acting workshops, small business workshops, management and marketing workshops, and personal success workshops.

✦ ✦ ✦

Information Superhighway - The Internet

The Information Superhighway may not be here in the exact form that the creators had planned, but it is, nonetheless, one of the best resources for fast and free information. It is like nothing else out there. You can type a simple phrase into a search engine and in response receive over a million pages. Regardless of what you need, the Internet has some amount of information that can be of help.

❖ ❖ ❖

Purchase Programs

Infomercials are everywhere, and some of them provide excellent programs that are proven to be beneficial and extremely helpful in getting people from where they are now to where they want to be. Speed reading, investing, weight loss, personal improvement, and many more programs, most of which come with a money-back guarantee, can help you get motivated and reach your long-term goals.

❖ ❖ ❖

What Have Your Friends Experienced?

Ask your friends about their past experiences. The more you understand about the experiences of those around you, the better you can learn from and build on your own experiences. Talk with your friends about what they have been through and the obstacles they have overcome.

❖ ❖ ❖

You will never find time for anything. you must make it.

Charles Buxton

Recommended Books

After reading an interesting or informative book look to the back for further recommendations and suggested reading. This is an easy way to continue learning about a subject you really enjoy.

What Have They Learned?

Ask your friends what they have learned about life in general. Do they have theories or philosophies about living a satisfying life? The best advice is communicated personally. This allows for questions, further explanation when necessary, and a more personal interaction. Ask your friends about their thoughts and beliefs, and you may come away with a great idea or two.

✦ ✦ ✦

Learn from Your Family

Interview your family members about their past and future. You're with them for life, and that means you can learn from them for life. Brothers, sisters, aunts, uncles, moms, dads, nieces, and nephews all have life experiences that can help others enjoy better lives. The only way you'll know if your family members have great information is to simply ask them.

✦ ✦ ✦

Your Radio Stations

Tune your radio to informational or resourceful stations. On a daily basis you will learn new and interesting facts, hear from experts on many different subjects, and increase your knowledge of the world around you.

✦ ✦ ✦

Newspapers

Subscribe to at least one newspaper. Keeping up on daily events and the world outside our front door is vital to a motivated and innovative mind. There are many choices in the marketplace. Take a look at the newspaper stand to find one that fits your needs.

Newspaper Clippings

When you come across a great article in the newspaper, clip it out and file it. Great stories can be easily lost if you don't do something about keeping them. While you read the paper, mark the corners of the pages containing good articles with a red 'x'. Put it aside until you are ready to cut and file. When you go back, page through to the marked sections, cut them out, and you'll have a large collection of great motivational articles in no time at all.

You will never find time for anything. you must make it.

Charles Buxton

✦ ✦ ✦

Share Your Findings

After you have learned something or read something in the paper that you'd like to share, tell your friends and co-workers about it. This will help to further ingrain the ideas into your mind.

✦ ✦ ✦

Magazines Subscriptions

If you don't want to subscribe to a newspaper, or would like a different type of medium to get your information, subscribe to a newsworthy magazine. These provide the same benefits as a newspaper subscription.

✦ ✦ ✦

Daily Events

Keep up on what is happening in the world. It may not directly affect you today, but the changes and events that take place in the world will affect you in time. Becoming aware of your environment and the people throughout the world will help you to get a full per-

Make a list of questions you would like answered. It doesn't matter if you look up the information immediately. Just take a minute or two to jot down the things that you have always wondered about. When the time is right, take out your list and start fact finding.

spective of life. You can watch the news programs, read newspapers and magazines, listen to the radio, or talk with your friends and co-workers about current events.

✦ ✦ ✦

Learn a New Language

Purchase books, tapes, or programs to learn a new language. You can also check these items out from the library to save money. If you know of a friend or family member that speaks a different language, get in touch with them and ask if they would be interested in helping you learn about their culture and language. This is a great way of stretching yourself beyond your current abilities and experiences.

✦ ✦ ✦

New Hobbies

Get involved with a new hobby. This can have an enormous effect on your motivation. Millions of people stop learning once school is finished, but your brain needs new information to function effectively. Starting a new hobby will give you the opportunity to start learning and getting excited again.

✦ ✦ ✦

Musical Instruments

Learn how to play a musical instrument. Music teaches timing, focused thought, dedication, hard work, and creativity. Children and adults alike should take up an instrument that they like and learn how to play it. You don't have to take lessons. Get your hands on some good learning manuals and lock yourself away in a soundproof room.

✦ ✦ ✦

Focusing In

The power of focus is unbelievable. When a person focuses their energy, amazing things happen. Confidence and self-esteem sky rocket, stress is reduced, motivation is peaked, attitude is improved, and the overall quality of life is enhanced. Choose a topic that you are passionate about and focus on becoming the best.

✦ ✦ ✦

Memory

Putting all of this new knowledge into your head is only important if it stays there and is readily available for you to use. This is why a good memory program is important. Many books and tape series have been created to help people retain and recall the information they learn. Knowledge is only power if you can remember what you've learned.

✦ ✦ ✦

Your Local University or Technical College

Enroll in a course at your local college. Instead of just being interested in something, take a class and really get involved in the topic. Visit Web sites, call, or go to the campus to obtain the necessary enrollment and tuition information.

✦ ✦ ✦

Enroll in a Night Course

If you work full-time and can't fit school into your schedule, night classes may be the answer for you. Many programs are available through universities and community colleges

The dictionary is the only place that success comes before work.

Anonymous

Your Children's Questions

When your kids ask you about something, give them the right answer. Some adults enjoy making up crazy stories about how things work when they don't know the truth. If your son or daughter asks you how something works do a little research and find out the real answers. This will teach you and your children about something new.

in nearly every city. After a little investigation on your part, you should be able to find many evening opportunities for furthering your education.

✦ ✦ ✦

Enroll in an Internet Course

In recent years, Internet courses have gained credibility and can offer you the convenience and the affordability you are looking for. If learning at home better suits your needs, check into courses online for more information.

✦ ✦ ✦

When You Don't Know the Word

When you come across a word that you don't know, look it up in the dictionary. If you just skip words and expressions that you don't know you'll never improve your vocabulary. Take the extra minute it takes to look up a word and start growing your vocabulary today.

✦ ✦ ✦

Calendars that Teach

Purchase a calendar that teaches you something each day. There are many products on the market that have a new word, interesting fact, or important event listed on each day. Without much effort, you will be able to learn something new every turn of the calendar.

✦ ✦ ✦

Five Minute Reading

Take five minutes each morning or night to read. Time is a scarce resource for many, but five minutes a day can fit into any schedule. If time permits, extend your reading to twenty or thirty minutes per day.

6

Motivation at Work

To create a satisfying and fulfilling career it is important to progress and grow in your position. With the right motivation tips in place, this task is simple. You will be able to accomplish more in less time, increase your chances for promotion, and leave the office feeling better about yourself and your work.

These tips will help to prepare you to make the most of your time at work. Whether you have a nine-to-five job at the office or work seventy hours a week as a CEO, these tips will get you motivated as soon as you walk through the doors.

Charts, Charts, Charts

If you are working on a project that includes numbers, track your progress with a large chart and hang it at your work station. If you are in sales, place a tally of your sales out in the open so you and everyone else can see them.

Go to Work with a Purpose

Make a mental or physical list of things you need to accomplish at work. Look over your list the night before you go to work. You can even review your list in the morning while you eat breakfast. This tip will save you an enormous amount of time because you'll know exactly what needs to be done as soon as you walk through the office doors.

✦ ✦ ✦

Have a Clock in the Office

Time is the most sacred resource we have. Keeping a clock in the office helps to keep you on track and motivated with your work.

✦ ✦ ✦

Work To-Do List

After you have compiled a task or project list, keep it in a close drawer or desk. Each time you accomplish an item, cross it out and move to the next item. Have the list clearly displayed in the office when you leave. In the morning, you'll come in, examine the list, and know exactly what needs to be accomplished.

✦ ✦ ✦

Keep Your Door Closed

Constant distractions can make getting things done very difficult. Simply shutting your door while you are busy is a great way to keep the distractions to a minimum. We all enjoy social interaction but when things need to be done on time, a little more focus may be necessary.

✦ ✦ ✦

Look to the Competition for Motivation

When you're in a slump at work, look to see how your competition is doing. The state of competing will create instant motivation. When you see another business accomplishing more and trying new things, you'll be motivated to do the same. You may even pick up some great ideas along the way.

+ + +

Give Yourself a Daily Start-Time

Create a time that you will start working each day. You may enter the office at eight o'clock, but the work doesn't always start at that time. Getting caught up in things and not starting to work until later in the day is common, but not if you create and stick to your morning start-time.

+ + +

Meet With Those Above You

Growth motivation (improving and increasing your skills, experience, knowledge, confidence, etc.) comes in great part, from the top. Get to know those above you in your organization. Discover what goals and desires they have for the future of the company as a whole, and for your division or function specifically. This will motivate you to progress within the company and demonstrate your ambition and work ethic to management.

What a wonderful life I've had! I only wish I'd realized it sooner.

Colette

7

Finding Your Passion

IT IS POSSIBLE TO DO WHAT YOU LOVE, and get paid for it. It won't come knocking on your door, and it won't be dropped into your lap. You have to make it happen. Because you will be spending a great deal of your time at work it is important that you enjoy and look forward to it.

The next section will show you how to find your passion and create a career out of that passion. Looking forward to work isn't an impossible dream. If you take the right steps, you can enjoy that feeling every morning.

Collect Eye Catchers

When you come across a picture, story, word, book, or anything that interests you, keep it. Many people have a very difficult time deciding on what they want to do with their lives, and for good reason. It's a very big decision and affects the bulk of your life. By collecting things that grab your attention you may realize where your true passion lies.

Look for eye catchers in:

- ✧ magazines
- ✧ newspapers
- ✧ newsletters
- ✧ books
- ✧ pictures
- ✧ photographs

What Do You Enjoy Doing?

Make a list of the things you like doing. It doesn't matter if you can think of a job that fits with the activity. You may have to bring several ideas together to form a career. The important thing is that you get a job that you like doing. If you can do this, then you will be leaps and bounds ahead of the majority of workers in the world.

✦ ✦ ✦

What Are You Good At?

What skills or talents do you currently have that could grow into a career? Make a list of everything you are good at, and you may just find a position geared specifically to that interest. Most often the things you are good at are also the things you enjoy doing the most.

✦ ✦ ✦

When Do You Feel Your Best?

Think about the times when you feel like you're at your best. What activities are you doing at that time? If you can narrow down the things you do that make you feel great, then you've made a lot of progress towards finding your passion. When you are at your best you will be more effective, confident, and creative in your work.

✦ ✦ ✦

When Do You Have Fun?

Make a list of the activities that you find fun and enjoyable to take part in. Anything goes when you're making this list. You may not see how it's possible to have fun and make a great living, but it's not only possible, it's probable. Knowing what you have fun doing will also make the decision making process easier. For example, if you love playing with kids you'll be able to focus your overall strategy towards children.

✦ ✦ ✦

The Get Up and Go

What would make you want to get out of bed? So many people don't look forward to getting out of bed and heading to work. It doesn't have to be that way! Think long and hard about what would make you eager to get up in the morning, and you'll be closer to finding your passion.

✦ ✦ ✦

Look for Experience

Once you have an initial list of interests, likes/dislikes, and activities that you enjoy doing, look around for others who are in that line of work or area. For example, if your list points to teaching others, talk to teachers in your area, or friends who have had experience in working with children. The more information you learn about your possibilities, the better choices you can make.

✦ ✦ ✦

Network

After searching around for experienced individuals you will be well on your way to creating an important network of peers. Keep in contact with the people you meet, and write down their contact information in a safe place. Once you delve deeper into your particular area, you'll find great value in a network of friends who are willing to help you get started.

To find out what one is fitted to do and to secure an opportunity to do it is the key to happiness.

John Dewey

Tangents to Success

You never know what is going to happen in the future. You could get a job at a recreation department, realize you love kids, and later become a teacher. You could work for a grocery store, notice the flower department, get transferred, start a small garden at home, and eventually open up your own flower shop. The important thing here is not knowing exactly what your future holds, but simply getting started. If you never start, you'll always be right where you are.

Keep Your Eyes Open

If you have an idea of what you would like to get into, keep your eyes wide open for any opportunities that match your passion. Perhaps a local organization is hiring for a position that would help you gain experience in your area. There may even be classes at the local university or technical school that cater directly to your interests.

✦ ✦ ✦

Work Turns to Fun

Work becomes fun when you do what you love. Use this sentiment as motivation to change careers. Playing it safe and comfortable isn't always the best thing for you in the end. If you would like to have fun and get paid for it, put time into creating a passionate career.

✦ ✦ ✦

The General Direction

In the early stages of the game, knowing the exact position or occupation you would like to have is not as important as finding an area that you enjoy or a general direction that you would like to pursue further. If you wait for the perfect position to appear, you may be waiting for a long, long time.

✦ ✦ ✦

You Can Always Change

This, more than anything else, holds people back from going after their goals, dreams, and passions; they are afraid it won't work. You will never be 100% guaranteed that anything you do will be 'the thing' for you. It's a risk, but with risk comes the chance for high returns. You could play it safe and stick with something you don't really enjoy. You could keep your ambitions and passions in your head, never letting them grow into something much bigger. But that's not what you're going to do. Take it slow, do it right, and you will end up exactly where you want to be.

✦ ✦ ✦

Take It Slow

The day after you realize what you love doing, is not necessarily the best time to quit your job and immerse yourself into your newfound interest. When making life changes, it is important to take it in steady, logical steps. Before you make any drastic changes, look into every option, every detail. Play it smart and you'll avoid many of the problems that individuals face when they act before they think things through.

✦ ✦ ✦

Are There Any Openings?

The first thing to look into after choosing a career path is a position opening. This should be done while you are at your current place of employment. If you cannot find an open position that fits your needs, you'll need to be patient and bide your time. You will also learn more about the industry and standards as you search for an offer.

✦ ✦ ✦

Don't Make a Move!

Before you even think of changing companies or careers, first ask yourself if things with your current employer can be improved

You only live once; but if you live it right, once is enough.

Adam Marshall

When I Grow Up . . .

What did you want to be when you were young? You may find that what you wanted years ago is what you still want today.

enough to meet your level of fulfillment and satisfaction. Your initial desire to leave a company that isn't making you happy could be a short-term problem. Meet with your supervisor or manager to see if changes can be made to your position. You may find that the perfect job is right under your nose.

✦ ✦ ✦

Learn, Educate, Research

Learn about your chosen field. This tip will not only help you to make informed decisions and become a better candidate for your position, it will also motivate you to make it happen. Educate yourself about the processes, skills, systems, and knowledge the job requires. The more you learn, the more you'll understand. The more you understand, the closer you will be to reaching your goal.

✦ ✦ ✦

Furthering Your Education

Look into college programs and tech schools in your area. If your new job requires a degree or post-high school education, you will need to know the details about the programs offered in your community. Before you can check into school programs you will have to look into the position to get a feel for what schooling or experience will be necessary.

✦ ✦ ✦

The Referral System

If your friends or family are affiliated with your chosen industry ask them about possible openings or important information. You may find out that the position you thought you wanted, is nothing like the picture you had

in your head. You may also find that it is better than you had imagined.

✦ ✦ ✦

Visit Businesses in the Area

If you are interested in becoming a chef, visit local restaurants to inquire about that position. The more you can learn during this time period the better. When your career and future are at stake, shortcuts are not advised.

✦ ✦ ✦

Leave On Good Terms

After you have chosen a field, learned about the position, and sought out openings and offers, make sure you leave your current employer on good terms. This is good advice for two reasons; you don't want to create ill will with those you have worked with, and you also don't know if you'll be returning to that position if you find that the new opening isn't what you were looking for.

✦ ✦ ✦

An Obstacle to Overcome

Safety and security play important roles in all of our lives. They keep us stable and free from harm. They can, however, overstep their boundaries and create a suffocating circle around us. If you have always dreamed of running your own business, then get the ball rolling and learn about it. If becoming a teacher is what you have always wanted to do, take classes or talk with others who have done the same. Do not stay where you are simply because you are afraid to change. You may not regret your decision to play it safe now, but you surely will when you are older.

First say to yourself what you would be; and then do what you have to do.

Epictetus

Maximize the Possibilities

Take part in as many different activities as possible. Try different hobbies. Join groups that sound interesting. Read books covering vastly different subjects. As you increase your personal experiences you will have a greater chance of finding your calling in life.

Family First

For some, this tip is a no-brainer. For others, this area becomes somewhat of a sticky situation. I personally believe that family should come before your career, and that is why it is vital to first check with them about the changes you plan to make. For instance, if there is an opening that requires a move, ask yourself, "Will this have a negative effect on my family?" If so, you may have to reevaluate your options.

✦ ✦ ✦

Work with the Numbers

When you change jobs, you will most likely also be changing your income. Before you make this leap into a new career, work with the numbers to see if you will be able to afford this transition. You may have to build your savings to make it work, or take on extra work. Either way, knowing what lies ahead is the key.

✦ ✦ ✦

The Library

Go to your local library and read every book you can get your hands on that deals with the new career you are beginning. If you need to know the skills necessary for the job or what the average income is for a beginning position, the library is a great place to start your search. It's free, at your fingertips, and ready and willing to help you with any aspect of the job.

✦ ✦ ✦

The List of Old

Get out a sheet of paper and a pen or pencil. Draw a line down the center of the paper. On the left-hand side, write *Advantages*, and on the right-hand side write *Disadvantages*. This list will comprise what you like and don't like about your current job. After filling out the columns you may realize that your current job is the place for you.

✦ ✦ ✦

The List of New

As you did with the previous tip, write out the disadvantages and advantages of the career you are hoping to begin. A decision of this magnitude must be worked out and broken down into its smaller parts. Talking with others who have made career changes, I have learned that impatience and impulsiveness are the two factors to avoid. Take your time to fully understand what you are looking for and what the market can offer you and your family.

✦ ✦ ✦

Things You Must Know

With most openings and offers for employment, a list of prerequisites accompanies the description. These are vital to your success. If you do not know what is required before and during your employment, the chances of you actually being accepted for the position are minimal at best. If the prerequisites are not listed, call the company for that information.

✦ ✦ ✦

Passion holds up the bottom of the universe and genius paints up its roof.

Chang Ch'ao

You Can Be Anything You Want to Be

You have probably told this to your children or friends at one time or another. It's time to listen to your own advice. If someone, somewhere has made a living doing what you want to do, then you can do it too. However impossible it may seem now you can be anything you want to be. With enough desire and belief in yourself anything is possible.

Make a Match

Make a list of companies that match your needs. After compiling a list of these businesses, investigate further to see which of the companies also have openings. This list will give you a great starting point for the initial contact and inquiry stages.

✦ ✦ ✦

The Daydream

What do you daydream about? This could be a good indicator of what you would like to do.

8

Risk & Failure: Making them Work for You

SOMETIMES MOTIVATION DECREASES not because of how much you want something but because of how much you don't want something. Sound a little confusing? A simple example will help to clear things up: Bob works in a manufacturing plant and has the motivation to do his job effectively and efficiently, and has a few ideas that might speed up production. Bob's ideas are excellent, but the fear of failure causes him to keep his ideas from his boss. This fear of failure transformed initial motivation to reluctance and doubt.

This example is common in today's workplaces, homes, and schools all across the country. Before motivation can take place, the fear of failure needs to be dealt with. The next section of tips will help you to realize the truth about failure and how to overcome it.

Your Risk Personality

It's important to know what type of risk taker you are. This will help to explain why you think the way you do, and that is the key to creating positive changes in your life.

✧ Risk-averse people do not take many risks. If it's not a sure bet, they won't gamble.

✧ Someone who is risk-neutral is indifferent about the risks involved in a situation.

✧ The other side of the spectrum is risk-seeking. These individuals look for risky situations. The greater the risk, the greater the return.

✧ Which type are you?

Research Your Fears Away

After a little bit of poking around in the newspaper or library, you'll come across many stories of men and women who, after failing hundreds of times, stuck with it and succeeded in the end. Persistence is the vital link. It isn't important if you succeed at your first attempt. The important thing is that you get up again and again when you fall. In the end, you will succeed.

✦ ✦ ✦

Without Failing, You Cannot Succeed

Succeeding the first time simply does not happen very often. What are the chances that you can try something new and do it successfully on the first try? With a little logical thought you'll realize that it doesn't work like that. Failing is just finding out what doesn't work so you can eventually find out what does work. It's narrowing down the vast amount of possibilities until you find the right one. It may be a needle in the haystack, but the needle is indeed there, and with enough effort and persistence you will find it.

✦ ✦ ✦

It's All in the Keys

Picture a grand piano sitting in front of you. Except for this enormous instrument, the room is empty of both objects and sound. It's just you and the keys. Also imagine that you don't know a thing about playing the piano. This may or may not be true, but for the purpose of our example, you have no inkling about how to play. If I asked you to play a 'C' note, you would most likely not get it right on your first try, but that's one less key you have to try on your next turn. As you go on failing, you'll actually be narrowing your choices for the successful key. In time, you will hit the correct key. The same is true for life. As you fail, you'll be defining what works and what doesn't. After failing for some time you'll end up playing the right key.

✦ ✦ ✦

Learn From Failing

Picture the piano example again, but this time you don't keep track of what keys you play. You hit a wrong one, and the next time you try you don't remember where the wrong one was, so you may hit it again. This is truly failing. If you do not learn from your mistakes, you will take nothing away from the experience. You must learn from failing. If you learn from each attempt you are succeeding.

✦ ✦ ✦

Study Each Attempt

If your goal is to stop being negative, study each failure. If you find yourself becoming negative at work, take the time to think about the causes of your negativity and what you can do to remedy the situation. After examining your failures you'll have a clear understanding of success.

✦ ✦ ✦

Focus on the Process, Not Results

Do not focus solely on outcomes. If you truly want to improve and learn from your mistakes, focus on the process. Golf is an excellent example. For months a friend of mine

> *A stumble may prevent a fall.*
>
> English Proverb

Face the Facts

If you want to change there is going to be some amount of risk involved. It may not work and you may fail, but that is life. You have to be willing to take some risks because that is the only way you can enjoy the returns life has to offer.

was trying to improve his score. That was his only objective from start to finish, and it didn't happen. Only when he focused on the process, the swing, did the score finally improve.

✦ ✦ ✦

Risks - A Must for Success and Happiness

Take risks. Life is too short to always play it safe. If you did this, you would be passing up opportunities that could make your life happier and more fulfilling. The fear of risk taking is the culprit in many unachieved dreams and goals.

✦ ✦ ✦

It's Not Forever

A great fear for many people is the fear that once they begin something new they will have to stick with it forever. The good news is, you can always start over, change, or scrap the whole idea. That's the great thing about life. You can always change.

✦ ✦ ✦

Make a List of Fears

You can't begin to solve your problems until you know what you are up against. It's time to make another list. Get out a sheet of paper, a pencil, and your honesty. Make a list of why you are afraid of proceeding with a particular goal, system, program, direction, change, or plan. For each item create a plan of action to tackle the problem and confront the fear.

9

Children & Motivation

I F THERE IS ONE THING that equals the importance of self-motivation, it is instilling in your children the skills necessary to get motivated and achieve their goals. Giving your children the tools to succeed is the goal of every parent.

This section contains tips and ideas to help you teach your children how to get and stay motivated. You will be offering them the tools to succeed today and in the future. Your children need to learn about motivation. Now you have somewhere to start.

Switch the Games

Instead of video games give your children games to play that help them mentally or physically. As children are inundated with games and television shows that offer no activity for their minds or bodies, our children are becoming physically and mentally worse off than those before them. Games that teach should always be within their reach. Here are a few ideas:

⋄ games from your childhood
⋄ game books from the library
⋄ have them make up games
⋄ ideas from teachers at school

Anything is Possible

Teach your children at a very young age that anything is possible. Simply stating this message to them throughout their lives is enough to make a major impact.

✦ ✦ ✦

Cut Down On T.V. Time

One of the habits that weigh down the motivation of people all around the world is watching an extremely large amount of television. Moderate amounts are fine, and larger amounts of informational and educational shows are great. Recent studies have shown that the average child watches nearly three to four hours of television per night. This will decrease anyone's motivation over a period of time.

✦ ✦ ✦

When It's Broke, Fix It

When you see a lack of motivation or drive in your child, step in. It may be difficult to bring this to their attention, but problems that go unchallenged will not go away on their own.

✦ ✦ ✦

The Activity Hat

When left to their own devices, even the most motivated children will resort to less helpful activities. In times like these, the *Activity Hat* is a great solution! Put together a list of ten to fifteen activities that your children can do. When they get bored, have them choose an activity from the hat.

✦ ✦ ✦

Hobby Opportunities

Get your children involved in a hobby. When you learn something very intimately, your confidence increases along with your knowledge and experience. Curiosity, motivation, and excitement all increase. The point behind hobbies and educational activities is to offer them as many outlets as you can that include the founding forces of motivation and goal achievement. Without their knowing it, a hobby teaches commitment, motivation, dedication, goal setting and achievement, a positive attitude, sacrifice for the greater and longer term good, hard work, and most importantly, the lesson of believing in yourself and realizing success.

✦ ✦ ✦

Offer Help with Their Hobbies

After your child finds a hobby that interests her, offer your help when she needs it. Go to the library to get her books on her subject. Take her to events that focus on her hobby. Talk to her about it. Listen to what she likes about it. Get interested, and your kids will do the same.

✦ ✦ ✦

Magazine or Newspaper Subscription

Let your children get a subscription to a magazine or newspaper. As the mind increases in experience and knowledge, motivation and curiosity do as well. The two go hand in hand. Seeing your kids interested in learning will more than make up for the small cost of a subscription.

A man never stands as tall as when he kneels to help a child.

The Knights of Pythagorean

Give Them Projects to Work On

Give your children fun projects to work on in the home or outside. If you want to get creative there are thousands of activities you could involve them in. From building blocks to building stories, the home is an excellent place for your children to get motivated about learning and growing as an individual. Try out these ideas:

✧ have an at home science fair
✧ write and illustrate their own story
✧ research and host 'nationality night'
✧ write and play their own songs
✧ write and perform their own plays

Library Trips

If you haven't been to the library lately, go. When you do, bring your children along for the ride. I have seen how an interest in learning and reading has turned people's lives around. Instill in them the desire to improve through learning and you will be giving them an extremely valuable gift.

✦ ✦ ✦

Monthly Celebration

Hold a monthly celebration for your children's accomplishments. You can recognize school achievements or progress with their personal goals. Showing appreciation and praising them for their hard work is central to keeping them motivated.

✦ ✦ ✦

Hindsight is Always 20/20

When you talk with your kids about their motivation, remember that things aren't as clear to them as they are to you. You have already lived as a child and have grown into an adult. The mistakes you see them making are obvious to you, but to a child it may seem like the right thing to do. Simply try to see things from their point of view, as a child, and you will be able to relate easier and make more of an impact in their lives.

10

Motivating Others

THE ABILITY TO MOTIVATE OTHERS is a valuable skill. Teachers, employers, coaches, and parents all require this rare ability. When you understand how to motivate other people, you will be able to help them reach their goals and their potential. It is a talent that everyone needs, but very few possess.

This chapter offers a beginner's guide to getting the best from other people. You will be able to get your students, kids, and employees excited and eager to succeed. By motivating others you will also better understand how to motivate yourself.

You are a Coach

When you work with other people remember that you are coaching them. If you start bossing them around or demanding things from them, the results will not be pleasant. It takes the right frame of mind to motivate others. See yourself as a coach whose success comes only through the success of your people. To practice these traits try the following activities:

- ◇ coach your child's sports team
- ◇ tutor kids
- ◇ mentor others at work

It All Starts with a Goal

Create specific and measurable goals. If you are a coach, manager, parent, teacher, or CEO of a million dollar company, the advice will stay the same. A goal creates a plan of action and gives you a great motivational tool to use. When you want to motivate others, first begin with a mutual goal.

❖ ❖ ❖

The Loss is Yours Alone

This tip will motivate both you and those you are trying to motivate. The responsibility of failure lies with the boss, coach, or teacher. This means that you have to do whatever you can to make sure your people succeed. When your people reach their goals, you can share in that excitement, but the full responsibility of failure is yours alone to accept.

❖ ❖ ❖

Share in the Victory

When your people achieve their goals, take a step back and let them bask in the glory. If you have a habit of taking credit for the success of your people, their motivation will decrease. They must feel important and worthy in order to stay motivated to keep producing excellent results.

❖ ❖ ❖

Make Your Praise Specific

In order for praise to have the desired effect it must be specific. Instead of saying, "Great job today," you could say, "Great job on making those three sales today." Specific praise lets the receiver know that you actually noticed them doing something well. Coaches who use general praise will not be able to motivate others through the use of recognition.

✦ ✦ ✦

Praise Immediately

Praise successes and good work soon after it occurs. The longer you wait to praise, the less impact it will have. If one of your kids is finally on time to dinner, but you don't tell him until later that night, the praise is too far separated from the action to have a positive effect. Instead, you should comment on his timeliness as soon as he sits down at the table.

✦ ✦ ✦

Be Sincere

Kids and adults alike can see right through insincere praise and compliments. Insincere praise will not motivate your people, it will create a negative backlash. They may come to resent your insincerity and decrease their effort and dedication.

✦ ✦ ✦

Praise Individually

Take your employee, child, student, or athlete aside and praise them individually. This is a great way to keep their motivation high. If you are sincere, specific, and quick with your praise, and you do it one-on-one, it will really make a positive impact. They will leave the room feeling better about themselves and their work.

✦ ✦ ✦

If any thing goes bad, I did it. If anything goes semi-good, we did it. If anything goes really good, then you did it. That's all it takes to get people to win football games for you.

Paul "Bear" Bryant

Communication is Key

What you say is not what they hear. This idea is very important to understand and accept. When you say, "Please do this and that," there is little chance that they understand what you said. Simply giving a command is not enough to guarantee successful idea transmission.

✧ look for nonverbal feedback
✧ have them restate the main points
✧ give time for questions
✧ ask questions
✧ keep your message simple

Growth Opportunities

Among the greatest motivators around, opportunity for growth is at the top of the list. This includes further education, promotion to a higher position, or a position change within the same ranks. Individuals want to grow as workers, students, and athletes, but also as people. Offering your people the potential for growth will go a long way in motivating them.

✦ ✦ ✦

Avoid Motivation through Fear

Motivation through fear is overused and ineffective. It will unfortunately continue to be used by those who want results quickly and easily without regard for the people who do the actual work. Fear motivates immediately but creates anger, frustration, disloyalty, and resentment. When an intimidating coach turns her back, her people will stop working hard because their motivation is not authentic. They work only to avoid negative consequences. This always leads to trouble down the road.

✦ ✦ ✦

Average Work Needs Recognition

As someone in charge of others, you are most likely a high achiever. When you are in this position you may think that only above average results deserve recognition and praise. This is common among mangers and coaches because they expect those under them to also be high achievers. The fact of the matter is, the majority of people are not high achievers and therefore average results must be recognized and celebrated. A great manager takes average workers and makes them great.

Negative Coaching

"I get noticed when I do something wrong." This is common and does considerable damage to motivation. Do you only give attention to those whom you coach when they mess up? Do you look for errors and mistakes in the work of others? If so, you need to realize that this is a motivation decreasing habit. If people are only recognized when they do something wrong they'll work to stay invisible from your reprimands.

✦ ✦ ✦

I Did a Good Thing!

When a student, employee, child or athlete comes to you looking for praise, give it to them! The tendency of most is to say, "Yes, that's great. Now get back to work." Coaches think that good work is expected and shouldn't have to be constantly praised. Wrong. If you want your people to work hard and produce results, then you must be willing to praise their efforts. When they come running to you for recognition, give them what they desire and you will have yourself a very motivated individual.

✦ ✦ ✦

Achievement Motivation

Personal achievement is at the center of intrinsic motivation. The inner motivation to succeed and achieve is alive in all of us, but it is the coach that must bring it out. Give your people the opportunity to achieve and they will be motivated.

✦ ✦ ✦

The greatest motivational act one person can do for another is to listen.

Roy E. Moody

Incentives

Offering your people incentives is another way to increase their motivation. An example is offering a raise for a certain level of work or giving free time to children if they behave during class. You must be careful with this form of motivation because effort may become totally dependent upon further rewards. Use incentives within a larger program of motivation through recognition and growth. If it is the sole motivating force your results will decrease over time. Several incentives include:

✧ time off
✧ financial bonuses
✧ promotion

Recognition Motivation

Just beneath achievement motivation is the motivation that comes from recognition. It's like a one-two combination. People are motivated to achieve and to have others recognize that achievement. Your job as coach is to keep your eyes open for any type of personal achievement and recognize it with praise. Do this, and your people will work to receive it again and again.

✦ ✦ ✦

Money Isn't Everything

Believe it or not, money isn't the strongest motivator for people. Motivating with money is like coaching through fear in that it gets quick results. As with most quick and easy methods, the effects are short-lived. You soon find yourself back to the drawing board. Money is a motivator, but it cannot be the only method of motivation in use.

✦ ✦ ✦

Get Excited for Them

Don't wait for your people to get excited about their achievements; you can do it first. If you get excited about their work and results, they will do the same. Think of the excitement and motivation you would like to see in your people and then personally demonstrate it. They will feed off your energy and make it their own.

✦ ✦ ✦

New Skills

Because growth is such a big motivator for people, offer opportunities to learn new skills. You could offer workshops or seminars to increase their knowledge, hold meetings with your people to teach them new ideas or techniques, or create a library of books that will further their education.

✦ ✦ ✦

Make Failing a Positive

The people you coach must not be afraid to fail. If they are, they will play it safe and hold back ideas that might not be sure bets. The only trouble is, a company or group needs innovation, creativity, and risk taking in order to succeed. Your people must feel that failing is acceptable as long as learning is the result. When people are allowed to take chances and fail without negative consequences, they will be motivated to work hard and try new things to help you succeed.

✦ ✦ ✦

Get Their Input

Most coaching is not done in a democratic fashion. That is to say, you are in charge and have the ultimate control. This doesn't mean that you can't take suggestions and advice from those below you. Having a voice in decisions increases a person's motivation because they have a say in what happens to them. You don't have to implement all of the suggestions you hear, but over time you will come across a few gems. You'll have new ideas to work with and a motivated group of people. That is a win-win situation.

✦ ✦ ✦

Track Results

Give your people feedback. Individuals must see what their efforts are producing, and if

Many people die with their music still in them. Why is this so? Too often it is because they are always getting ready to live. Before they know it, time runs out.

Oliver Wendell Holmes

Show an Interest in the Person

This isn't the whole process of motivation, but it is an important one. Get to know the people you coach. Learn about their lives and what they want to accomplish. This will help you to coach them better and will let them know that you actually care about their well-being. After a sincere appreciation for your people is demonstrated, respect and motivation will follow.

- ⬦ ask about their family
- ⬦ know about their past
- ⬦ know about their plans for the future
- ⬦ what do they like
- ⬦ what do they dislike

they need to make corrective changes. A great way to give feedback is to keep track of measurable goals. For example, if you coach a team of salespeople, you could post weekly sales for each person around the office. This will let them know where they stand and will motivate them to keep progressing. Let people know how they are doing, give them the resources to improve, and recognize their progress.

✦ ✦ ✦

The Lazy Factor

If you start something, see it through. A common mistake of coaches is to start a program and fire people up, only to get lazy and let the program dissolve. After time, whether you are committed or not, your people will expect you to let new programs slide, and their motivation won't increase. The point is simply this; if you want motivated workers, you must be motivated yourself.

✦ ✦ ✦

Questions???

Your people must feel free to ask questions. If you create a 'speak when spoken to' environment, you will not only have unmotivated people, but you will most likely have very unhappy and angry workers or students.

✦ ✦ ✦

Open Door Policy

Keep your time open for employees, kids, students, and athletes. You obviously can't devote all of your time to talking with others, but the easier it is to speak with you about problems or solutions, the easier it will be for your people to succeed. This is a tangible representation of coaching your people instead of simply bossing them around. If you see yourself as a coach helping others to succeed, you will want your people to have access to you at all times.

✦ ✦ ✦

The Vision

This isn't as simple as the other tips contained in this book, but it is important and should be mentioned. For a truly motivated workforce or group of individuals you must create a vision for the future. Your people must have something to believe in and follow collectively. They need an idea or value that brings them together for a common goal. If you don't create a vision, you will not have a team working together, but a group of individuals thinking and working independently.

✦ ✦ ✦

How They Fit into the Vision

If you really want to create motivation with your vision, let your people know how they fit into the plan and how their unique abilities will help to make it happen. This will make them feel a part of the team and will change their focus from 'me' to 'us'.

✦ ✦ ✦

Security

Let your people know that they are secure. If the people you coach don't know if they'll be around tomorrow, their motivation will most likely not be favorable. They will be too worried about being replaced or fired. When your people are secure in their positions, they will

Motivation is everything. You can do the work of two people, but you can't be two people. Instead, you have to inspire the next guy down the line and get him to inspire his people.

Lido Anthony "Lee" Iacocca

Whose Side are You On?

Make it clear from the beginning that you are on their side. If you have to meet with an employee or student about a problem, don't blame or point fingers. Also, try not to create the us vs. them mentality. In your conversation create a feeling of working with your employee or student to find a solution.

focus on their job and how they can improve their skills.

✦ ✦ ✦

The Right Rewards

What gets rewarded gets done. This is a very powerful idea in coaching others. If you want your people to do certain things, reward them when they do those things. It sounds easy, but it's not. For example, an unruly child getting yelled at may not sound like a reward, but if that's the only attention they receive, chances are they'll do it again. You must be careful not to reward negative behavior. When you reward the right behavior, you'll have motivated people working with you and not against you.

✦ ✦ ✦

Consistency Counts

Be consistent with the people you coach. A lack of motivation can result from unequal pay for equal work. This is an obvious example, but one that may not be so obvious is giving out explanations or praise to the first in line and getting progressively less excited or involved as you go down the line. When you enter the doors and have energy, the first person you see will most likely get the best of you. As each person down the line greets you, they may not get the same energy from you. You may be tired of saying the same things twenty times, so a thorough explanation turns into a brief phrase. This brings the employees or students at the end of the line down and can decrease their motivation and effort. Be consistent with your people.

✦ ✦ ✦

Avoid Micromanaging

You assign a project, give your people the tools necessary to do good work, make yourself available for help and advice, and let them do it. That is the beginning of a healthy process. Unfortunately, many coaches do the first three steps and then proceed to stick their nose into every part of the project and ultimately do it themselves. Talk about killing motivation! Let your people do their work and help only when needed.

✦ ✦ ✦

Handling Change

You are working peacefully at your desk and your boss walks in. After saying hello and asking about your day, she begins to walk away and adds, "Oh yeah, I forgot to mention that there will be a 10% pay cut effective next week." What?! Do not drop bombs on your people and then walk away. If you have negative news or will be making changes that affect your people, be prepared to gather them together for an informational meeting. Let them know the details of the situation and what needs to be done in response. If your people understand why changes occur they will be less likely to resist them. Take time to let them know changes are coming and why they are necessary.

✦ ✦ ✦

Keep Them Updated

Keep your people updated about changes that happen within the company, their department, or their position. This is both a security and trust issue. If they know about

Be kind, for everyone you meet is fighting a harder battle.

Plato

Tangible Recognition

Try offering these rewards to your people to show your appreciation and support:

- ✧ plaques
- ✧ company jacket
- ✧ pins
- ✧ trophies
- ✧ employee or student of the month certificates

changes that are coming, they will be able to prepare themselves and will respect you for your honesty.

✦ ✦ ✦

Goal Comparison

Have your employees, students, athletes, or children write down the goals they think you want them to achieve. Next, write out the goals you want them to achieve. After both lists are finished, meet and compare. You may be surprised to find that the goals don't always match. After a little restructuring and coaching, you'll be able to get everyone on the same wavelength.

✦ ✦ ✦

Reviews and Assessments

There are mixed feelings on reviews and assessment sessions, but overall I think they are beneficial. The problems arise when this is the only time you communicate with your people, or if you don't follow through on the goals and ideas that result from the meeting. Use performance reviews and appraisals to help make your people better and not to blame them for poor work.

✦ ✦ ✦

See Things from Their Point of View

Picture yourself in the shoes of the one you are trying to motivate. Many times a coach or boss will think in their terms only, forcing thoughts and commands into the heads of unsuspecting students. Before you coach others, try to look at things from their viewpoint. This will help you to better motivate them because you will be relating to their environment and experiences.

✦ ✦ ✦

Start with a Positive

In the realm of coaching for success, discipline plays an important role. If you are in a position of authority, you most likely have to take corrective actions. When you do so, try to begin with a positive. This ensures that the other person won't jump to a defensive position. It also allows your message to reach the listener. If you begin by explaining how they messed up, they will most likely stop listening and start getting defensive.

✦ ✦ ✦

What Motivates Them?

Ask your children what motivates them. This simple and direct approach can bring many factors to your attention that you may have never considered. If you know what gets them excited it will make your job as a parent much easier.

✦ ✦ ✦

Reward Team Efforts

If you want double motivation, reward the accomplishments of the team. You will be motivating each individual in the group and the team members will motivate one another.

Things turn out best for the people who make the best of the way things turn out.

John Wooden

SECTION TWO
Goals

11

Setting Goals

BEFORE ANYTHING HAPPENS, a plan must be created. Running out the door and going, going, going won't really help you if you don't know where you are going in the first place. Of the people who do have goals, many are frustrated and ready to give up because they haven't planned their goals correctly. When you set your goals using the right systems, you are already well on your way to reaching them.

The tips that follow will take you from the beginning to the end of the goal-setting process. When finished, you'll have a set of goals that are effective and efficient. When you set your goals properly, half of the work is already done.

The Beginning

When you are just beginning the goal setting process ask yourself the following questions:

- ✧ What do I want?
- ✧ How do I go about getting it?
- ✧ Who can help me?
- ✧ What can help me?
- ✧ What obstacles will I face?
- ✧ How will I deal with those obstacles?
- ✧ What do I have to change or give up?
- ✧ When do I want to accomplish my goal?

Take Inventory

Before you begin to set goals for the future, take inventory of where you are currently. For example, if you are creating financial goals, how much money do you now have in your savings account? Checking? What amount do you have planned for a college fund? This will help you set smart goals that will be both effective and powerful.

✦ ✦ ✦

Challenging

To be effective and motivating, your goals must be challenging. If you can achieve something with little to no effort, the challenge and excitement of the process will disappear. You are left with no interest in the goal. Create goals that make you stretch your abilities and push your limits.

✦ ✦ ✦

Achievable

The flip side of making your goals challenging is to make them achievable. If you are currently writing five pages a night for your novel, don't increase the amount to fifty pages. That simply isn't reasonable and will only serve to frustrate you. You have to look at the situation honestly and plan accordingly. With an increased amount of effort, could you achieve your goal? If not, lower the mark.

✦ ✦ ✦

Write Down W.I.F.M.

What's in it for me? If you cannot clearly and easily state why you have a goal, you will not reach it. You have to desire your goals in order for motivation to take place. There is no magic here. If you do not truly desire something, setting a goal to get it won't result in anything. When you aren't feeling very motivated to keep going, you can refer to your list of reasons for a reminder and immediate motivation.

✦ ✦ ✦

Write It Down

Write down your goals. Get out a sheet of paper and a pencil and get to work. When you think about your goals you don't really make a great deal of progress. Only when you write out a specific goal and plan of action do the wheels in your mind start creating solutions and opportunities.

✦ ✦ ✦

Use the Computer

Use your computer to plan out your goals. The computer offers many benefits. You can type in the information and edit it with relative quickness. You can also quickly save and retrieve your files.

✦ ✦ ✦

Print Your List

If you have made a list of goals on your computer, printing out the list will make it accessible at all times. You can even make multiple copies to carry with you throughout the day. Place all of your goal sheets in one binder to keep them organized and readily available.

✦ ✦ ✦

Think Out Loud

When goals are on the brain, as they should be constantly, think aloud. See how they

My goal is simple. It is the complete understanding of the Universe.

Stephen William Hawking

The Road Trip to Success

Setting a goal that has a good chance of success is like planning a trip across the country. The more detailed you make your vacation plans, the smoother things will go for you. If you don't take into account a budget, a map, or driving time you'll end up far from your desired destination. It is no different with your goals. Pay attention to detail and create a map that will guarantee you will arrive successfully.

sound when you say them to yourself. This will help you define your goals more precisely and become excited about the future.

✦ ✦ ✦

Building Blocks

To make your goals manageable, think about how they are put together. What are the different areas that need to be completed before the entire goal is finished? For example, if you want to go back to school you have to consider getting admission information, gathering together the funds for tuition, and deciding what path to take.

✦ ✦ ✦

Time

If you are dealing with a goal whose structure is time-based, break down each segment into a given time period. For example, if your goal is to start a small business within two years, break the steps into groups of months. This will allow you to enjoy constant short-term successes while coming closer and closer to your ultimate goal.

✦ ✦ ✦

Steps

A goal that consists of several steps needs to be treated much differently from other goals. Each step needs to be given its own plan and deadline. If your goal is step-oriented, make sure to treat each section as a goal in itself.

✦ ✦ ✦

Number

If your aim is a particular number like money raised or cigarettes reduced, break your goal down into smaller portions. Raising $10,000 may seem a little overwhelming, but collecting $100 for 100 days is much easier to manage.

✦ ✦ ✦

Break It Down

Nearly every goal that you will plan in your life should be broken into parts. Frustration often occurs because people try to tackle an enormous goal all at once. It's like trying to build a house all in one day. This isn't the way to go. Take your goal and break it into smaller, sub-goals. After you have done this, you will see that completing the project is possible. You will also get motivated from the short-term successes.

You can't hit a target you cannot see, and you cannot see a target you do not have.

Zig Ziglar

✦ ✦ ✦

Plan Each Section

When you break your goal down into sub-sections, be sure to give each section a plan of action. For example, if your goal is to live a healthier lifestyle, you may have several sections: diet, exercise, reducing stress, attitude, etc. Each section needs to be detailed in order to make it manageable.

✦ ✦ ✦

Financial Goals

Financial goals are key to a healthy and happy life. As long as you do not let money control your life or your ambitions, increasing your financial position is a great way to improve your circumstances. Without a plan, you will not be where you want to be as far as your wealth is concerned. Items on your list could include savings, money for vacations, or a college fund.

Write Your Goal in a Positive

State your goals in positives instead of negatives. For instance, replace the goal "I want to stop eating junk food," with, "I want to start eating healthier foods." This is an easy way to start the goal process on a positive note.

Health Goals

All the money in the world will be of no use to you unless you are alive and well. That is why health goals are vital to a fulfilling life. Include in your list: exercise, a balanced diet, ample sleep, less stress and any other goals that are applicable to you and your health.

✦ ✦ ✦

Relationship Goals

Very few people think to set goals to better their relationships with others. This is a mistake. You do treat these types of goals differently, because the outcome is a more fulfilling relationship, not a number or object. Regardless, you need to take inventory of where your relationships stand and create a plan to improve them.

✦ ✦ ✦

Happiness Goals

Everyone has a few personal goals that, when reached, will greatly increase their happiness. Personal goals are things that you have always wanted to do, but couldn't find the time or resources to do them. Most often, these types of goals do not include financial success. Starting a new hobby, reading more books, or joining a pottery class are examples of happiness goals.

✦ ✦ ✦

Self-Actualization Goals

Self-actualization is reaching your potential. It is becoming what you know you can become, and doing what you know is in your power to accomplish. Often times, these goals mix with the other types. For example, becoming the president of your company is both a self-actualization goal and career goal. Do not be afraid of setting lofty goals. Dreaming is very important in life. You may not reach the top of every mountain, but the dream of doing so will help you reach heights never before experienced.

✦ ✦ ✦

Career Goals

Do you love your job? If not, then a list of career goals is required. This encompasses salary, position, potential for promotion and development, etc. You can also think about your passion and how to go about making it a part of your daily life.

✦ ✦ ✦

The Biggest List in the World

Creating lists is a major part of goals and improvement. Try making a list of everything you have ever wanted. The wishes can transcend all categories, and can be as small or as large as you wish. It is much easier to think outside the box when you go about your list creating with no pressure, stress, or deadline. Enjoy this as an opportunity to dream a little. When finished, edit your list and prioritize.

✦ ✦ ✦

Read for Ideas

The book you are currently reading may give you a few ideas about goals you would like to accomplish. This happens with many other books. When you are reading your books, jot down goal ideas as they come to you. Some of the best goals are created from an idea you read in a book.

A man without a goal is like a ship without a rudder.

Thomas Carlyle

Goal Setting Software

If you like using your computer to help you solve problems, why stop when it comes to your goals? Throughout the Internet there are many sites offering goal setting programs. You type in the required information and the program creates a plan of action for you.

Watch for Ideas

If used correctly, television is an excellent resource. As you watch, each area of your life is represented on the screen. You may see a character who has a job you would like. Jot it down. Perhaps you are watching a movie and in it a character loves to jog. If this makes you think about jogging yourself, write it down.

✦ ✦ ✦

If at First You Cannot Think, Think Again

You may be in the mood for goals, but your mind can't think of anything good. That's fine. You can always come back later to rethink them. This is important to realize because many people only try things once. If you decide to work on goal setting on an off-day, you may never realize how much you could achieve with the use of goals.

✦ ✦ ✦

Brainstorm into a Tape Player

A great way to get your ideas down is to use your voice and a tape player. Press record and start thinking. You can do this anywhere you want, any time you want. While in the car at a stop light you may get an amazing idea but have nowhere to record it. With a tape recorder handy your problem is solved. You can also speak much faster than you can write which will allow you to get a lot of information down very quickly.

✦ ✦ ✦

Brainstorm with a Friend

Double the ideas! Ask a friend to have a little brainstorming session for a particular goal you are trying to achieve. You never know what experiences or knowledge others have until you involve them in the process. After a fun time brainstorming with someone else, you'll have a list that is not only twice as big but with ideas coming from a totally different viewpoint.

✦ ✦ ✦

An Ever-Changing List

A list is not set in stone. Some people feel trapped by their goals and wish lists. You can always go back to your lists and take items off, or add new ones. Your lists will change and that is a great sign of progress.

✦ ✦ ✦

Prioritize

Whether you are working on your health goals or career goals, or any other list that you have created, prioritize. Knowing your priorities is important because it decides where your time will be spent. There are very few resources as valuable as your time. This will ensure that the most important items receive attention first.

✦ ✦ ✦

A Friend to Proof

Give your list to a trusted friend. This may be difficult for many, and if it is for you, make a list containing only those items that you feel comfortable sharing. Letting a friend look over your list will help you weed out less de-

Give me a stock clerk with a goal and I'll give you a man who will make history. Give me a man with no goals and I'll give you a stock clerk.

J.C. Penney

When you set a goal you will:

◆ achieve more
◆ improve your performance at work
◆ increase your motivation
◆ develop a positive attitude
◆ increase your confidence
◆ increase your pride and satisfaction in your work

sirable goals and maybe even add a few that you may have overlooked.

◆ ◆ ◆

Ask Others About Their Goals

Other people's goals and desires are a great resource for you to learn from. Ask them what they plan on doing, or what they have already done. Maybe you'll get an idea you never thought of, or you'll get motivated about a story of success from a friend. You don't have to set your goals alone. You'll also make your friend feel important by giving attention to what they want in life instead of what you want.

◆ ◆ ◆

Make a Goal Binder

If you really want to make changes in your life, file all of your information, lists, and notes into a goal binder. From notes you jotted down after talking with a friend, to stories you read in magazines, keeping everything in one place will give you more power in goal setting. How? Imagine that you are trying to get in shape. As you are writing out the plan, you realize that while working on a recent goal you saved an article about health and fitness. Presto! Another piece of informational motivation to help you achieve your goal.

◆ ◆ ◆

Long-Term Goals

Set goals that will take you several months or years to achieve. When you set long-term goals, short-term failures won't hold you back. You may stumble here and there, but you know that a greater good lies ahead. This will help keep your motivation and attitude going strong throughout the valleys of the goal process. Another benefit of long-term goals is direction. When you have a vision of where you are heading it helps to qualify short-term decisions. You can ask yourself, "Does this short-term change fit with my overall goal or strategy?"

✦ ✦ ✦

Short-Term Goals

Create goals that can be accomplished within a few days or weeks. Small changes, each and every day, can change your life. It is the small things that you do constantly and consistently that will make up who you are. Many people think that taking small steps is too easy and little to make any improvement. That isn't true. If you learn to utilize your short-term thinking and actions, you'll be amazed at how much you can achieve. It is what you do every day that counts.

✦ ✦ ✦

Revisit Your Goal List & Edit

After you have written down your goals, leave them for several days and return to the list for editing. You'll be amazed at how a few days can help you think of new ideas, or make slight change to the goals you have already written down.

✦ ✦ ✦

Deadlines

Give every goal a deadline. Without a deadline, you can put it off forever. This is the killer of thousands of well-intentioned objectives. Each goal must have it's own timeline. This will serve as constant motivation because each day that goes by brings you closer and

The most important thing about having goals is having one.

Geoffrey F. Abert

Physical Benefits

Using goals can even improve your health. Research has shown that people who use goals effectively:

◇ suffer from less stress
◇ concentrate better
◇ have less muscle tension

closer to your deadline. Give each goal a date or time when you will finish. Remember to make it both challenging and achievable.

✦ ✦ ✦

When Will You Begin?

Give each goal a start date. This often overlooked aspect of goal setting is just as important as setting a deadline. Once you have created a great plan of action for your goal, without a time to start you could let it go weeks or even months before you pay any attention to it. By that time your motivation has decreased to such a low level that the goal is rarely pursued. You need to set a time when you will begin and stick to it. Procrastination is common among individuals who can't seem to reach their goals and this is a quick tip to overcome that problem. Your start date must also be challenging and achievable.

✦ ✦ ✦

Make Your Timeline Specific

March 15th, 2004. This is a specific deadline. Stating your start date as sometime next year isn't clear enough. That would give you ample time to procrastinate and put the effort off until it is too late. Specificity is key to motivation and ultimate success. The more specific your timeline is, the more work it can do for you.

✦ ✦ ✦

Plan Ahead

When you set deadlines for goals, be sure to take into account future activities. For example, if you will be on vacation during the month of July, you shouldn't set your deadline during that month. Check your calendar to ensure that you will be able to keep your plan intact.

✦ ✦ ✦

Specific Goals

Make your plan of action specific. This is one of the most important parts of the goal setting process. Nearly every goal that is accomplished is clear and detailed. Being specific helps in many ways throughout the goal process. It helps you use your time wisely. When you know exactly what needs to be done you won't waste your time heading in the wrong direction. It is a great motivator. When you make your goal specific you can begin to see how it will actually happen. Writing a book and getting it published may seem too difficult to tackle, but when all of the steps are laid out in front of you it becomes very possible. For example, if you wanted to vacation sometime in the future you could write down that you will take a vacation and leave it at that. You could also write that you will travel for two weeks in Italy from January 7 to January 21, spending no more than $3,000. The more specific you can make your plan of action, the better.

✦ ✦ ✦

He turns not back who is bound to a star.

Leonardo daVinci

Specific Sub-Goals

Along with the overall goal, make your subgoals specific. Using the above example, you could improve upon the vacation plan by writing the exact destinations you will visit in Italy and for how long. Give your subgoals their own timelines, making sure they are challenging and achievable. Plan out each

S.M.A.R.T. Goals

Does your goal satisfy each element? If not, reexamine your goals and make changes where necessary. This is an easy way to measure the effectiveness of each goal you have.

✧ Specific
✧ Measurable
✧ Attainable
✧ Relevant
✧ Timely

step and you will have motivation, understanding, and enthusiasm.

✦ ✦ ✦

Learn What You Need to Learn

With each goal or sub-goal you have, make a list of the skills and abilities that are required of you. Once you see what you will need to learn or experience, reaching your goals will not be a confusing matter. For instance, if you set a goal to become a singer and wish to have CD's and millions of dollars, there are some things you need to know first. How to sing, where to sing, for whom to sing, how to get a record contract, etc. The more you know, the better your chances for success will be.

✦ ✦ ✦

Contacts

Make a list of the people and organizations you need to contact. If you are an aspiring author, you would probably need to get in touch with writer's workshops, writing seminars, authors you may know, and any other person or group that can help you. Bringing outside resources in will help you with your plan.

✦ ✦ ✦

Don't Overdo It

Goals are the key to a healthy and happy life, but as with most things, only in moderation. Setting too many goals could be worse than not setting any at all. If you set too many goals for yourself, you will not be able to give any one goal the attention it requires. Having several goals is fine, as long as you can give each the time and effort they need.

Conflicting Goals

When you set more than one goal to work on, you could run into the conflicting goals dilemma. If working towards one goal hurts the progress of another, you may have to re-evaluate your choices. For example, if one goal is to spend more time with your family, and another is to advance in your career, you may find obstacles along the way because these two goals work in opposite directions.

To follow, without halt, one aim: there's the secret of success.

Anna Pavlova

❖ ❖ ❖

Measurable Goals

Your goals must be measurable. You have to be able to see and track your progress as time goes on. This will help you set good goals. Imagine your goal is to be happier. That is extremely difficult to measure. Instead, you will need to set goals such as getting a promotion or getting in shape. These goals can be measured. If you can measure your goal you will have the motivation that comes from little successes along the way. You will also be able to see how you are doing at each stage, and if changes need to be made.

❖ ❖ ❖

Short, Mid, and Long-Term Goals

One goal you have can actually be split into three main sections: now, soon, and later. This is another way of breaking down your goals, but from a different angle. For a business executive, a long-term goal could be increasing profits. The mid-term goals could be lowering costs and boosting sales. Finally, the short-term goals could be saving costs on production, quality, and training. The long-term

A, B, C

A great way to prioritize your lists is to apply letters to each goal. *A* goals are immediate and very important to you. *B* goals are important, but are not as time sensitive. Putting these off for a little while won't do much harm. *C* goals are the least important and can be put off for some time. Focus on your *A*'s.

goal keeps you focused and heading in the right direction while the mid and short-term goals give you something to work on each day.

✦ ✦ ✦

Make Yourself a Goal Tool Kit

Materials: Five sheets of paper, five pieces of tape, 1 black pen or marker, a dreamer's perspective. Take a goal you have in mind, any goal at all. With your pen or marker, write the goal, specifically, on each sheet of paper. Once this is complete, tape the goal in five places within your car, home, or office where you will frequently pass by. This will remind you of your goal on a daily basis.

✦ ✦ ✦

Sign Up for E-Zines

The Internet is filled with electronic newsletters (E-zines) that are geared towards goals; how to set them and reach them. Search the Web for these topics and sign up for several E-zines.

✦ ✦ ✦

Goal Web Sites

Along with E-zines, the Web is home to millions of sites that are in existence simply to help you reach your goals. Using a search engine or directory, type 'goals', or a phrase containing the word, into the search box. You'll find several Web sites that offer excellent goal-setting resources that will help you succeed.

12

Reaching Goals

AFTER YOU HAVE LEARNED how to set goals, the next stage is actually achieving them. This is the tricky part, but with the right information it is more than manageable. Achieving the goals you have put your time and energy into setting is a complex and trying process, but this will add to your excitement and enjoyment when you finally accomplish them.

As with all things, these tips and ideas work when you do. There is no secret to success or motivation. It takes dedication and hard work. If you can offer that to your goals, then your goals will give you everything you want in return.

Nightly Numbers

For number-based goals, track your daily results before you go to bed. This will keep the goal in your mind while you sleep as well as give you a reminder of your goal and progress every day.

The System of Success

Here is a complete goal setting and planning example that you can use to reach your goals. Like everything else, it works best when you do. Each part is covered in more detail throughout this section, but putting the steps together will help you to see the big picture.

✦ ✦ ✦

1. Goal

It all starts with a goal. For our purposes here, my goal is to start and finish a ten mile run sponsored by the city. The event will be held in August. Let's say that I can currently run five miles. Therefore, my specific goal is to improve my current distance by five miles.

✦ ✦ ✦

2. WIFM

Why do I want to accomplish this goal? This is a personal achievement goal with a slight health goal twist. I will feel like I met a challenge head on and came out successfully. I will also be pushing my limits and growing physically, mentally, and emotionally. Along with the personal victory, my health will improve due to the daily exercise.

✦ ✦ ✦

3. Plan of Action

My plan is to run five miles a day for seven days. Each week I will increase my distance by half a mile. If I find that I cannot complete my designated amount, I will make adjustments where necessary. Using the numbers above, it will take me ten weeks to reach my goal. Allowing for deviations, the schedule is set for twelve weeks of training. Along with running, the plan of action includes research and education. I need to learn about the techniques behind running long distances. I will go to the library and read about the topic, talk with others who have taken part in the run in past years, and look for experts in the field for information and advice.

✦ ✦ ✦

4. Deadline

The deadline is easy in this case. The run will be held on August 15, at nine in the morning.

✦ ✦ ✦

5. Measure & Record

Each day that I run I will mark the distance on a chart. The chart will start with five miles and reach to ten. Along the bottom will be the weeks leading up to the event. When the event arrives, you'll be ready.

✦ ✦ ✦

It's Goal Time

Set up a time each week to review the progress and upcoming steps of your goals. This is a great way to keep up with your goals, adjust as needed, and build your confidence by recognizing your successes.

✦ ✦ ✦

What's Working?

When you come across a tip or idea that really helped you, make a note of it. It just may serve to help you the next time around. Each tip and technique that is out there won't necessarily work equally for everyone. Some

Anywhere, provided it be forward.

David Livingstone

Make a Goal Bracelet

Materials: Bracelet, three to five charms. Break your goal down into smaller, sub-goals. Use the charms to represent each section. As you accomplish a level, add the charm to your bracelet. Once your goal is complete, you will have a full charm bracelet. For example, if your goal is to sell one-hundred products, you could have five charms representing twenty sales each. As you sell twenty products, you would add a charm. Continue until the entire bracelet is completed.

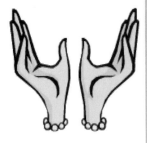

people respond better to certain ideas than others. That is why you must learn what motivates you and what doesn't. As you learn more about yourself, you will find that achieving success and happiness is much easier work.

✦ ✦ ✦

What's Not Working

Not only do you need to know what works, but also what doesn't work well for you. If you try out a tip and it doesn't work the first time, give it a second try. If after that you still don't like it, make a note of the situation and move on to something else. Many people don't learn from their previous mistakes and always start at square one with each goal. If you realize what works and what doesn't, you'll always be starting in a better position than you did previously.

✦ ✦ ✦

Chart It

If you have chosen a measurable goal, one that can be broken down into increments, using a small hand-written goal chart will work wonders for your motivation, attitude, and confidence. As you move along with your goals, mark your progress on the chart. You will see that, despite small dips here and there, the overall line is heading up. If you find that the line is continuously dropping, you will be able to make changes accordingly.

✦ ✦ ✦

Measure with a Checklist

If the goals you have set for yourself don't work well with a chart, you can use a checklist in its place. Just list the steps that you need to accomplish with a box next to each item. When you finish the step, place a check mark in the box. The sections you use are up to you. You can have a column for deadlines, start dates, plans of action, rewards, etc.

✦ ✦ ✦

Share Your Success

Sharing your success with others is an excellent way to keep your energy and motivation up throughout the entire goal process, as long as it is done right. You don't want to brag about your accomplishments, but telling your close friends and family about the things you are working on is perfectly acceptable.

✦ ✦ ✦

Small Successes = A Successful Life

It is the small things that we do each and every day that make up the whole of our life. Because of this, small changes and successes should be your focus. If you can make small improvements you are well on your way to making enormous changes in the long-run.

✦ ✦ ✦

If It's Broke, Fix It

If you find that part of your plan of action isn't working well, change it. Goals work well when you can work well. If a change needs to be made in order for your progress to run smoothly, don't be afraid to make it. Problems arise when the plan starts to take control instead of the person who created it. If you created it, you can and should make adjustments. There are no rules, no guidelines that you must follow. The control is in your able hands.

This one step, choosing a goal and sticking to it, changes everything.

Scott Reed

Place an 'X' on Your Calendar

Like counting down the days to your favorite holiday, you can use your calendar and a marker to help you reach your goals. As you move closer and closer towards your deadline, draw an 'x' through each day as it passes.

Buddy Up

Maybe someone at work is interested in getting in shape, or a neighborhood friend is trying to save money for a vacation. If so, buddy up with these people to double the efforts in the goal process. Two heads are better than one, especially when it comes to success. Trying to do everything by yourself is difficult and can be a bit lonely. Get others involved, enjoy the process, and get excited about the future.

✦ ✦ ✦

A Goal Mentor

You will soon become a goal expert. All of this information that you are digesting will be of use to everyone around you. Share your ideas, teach your children, help your friends and family. This will teach you more than any other learning process.

✦ ✦ ✦

Guaranteed Action

A great way to motivate yourself is to set up a situation that forces you to act in a particular way. Imagine that you are asked to give a speech at your annual work party. To ensure motivation you tell everyone that you are going to present an excellent speech. Now that you said it, you have to come through. This is an example of making the promise and being motivated to make it happen so you can keep your word.

✦ ✦ ✦

Fatal Questions

You just started a new goal; to stop smoking. The first thing many people do, which leads to their ultimate failure, is ask themselves defeating questions such as, "How can I do this?" Avoid asking yourself negative questions when you first set your goals. How much you believe in your ability to succeed plays an important role in your motivation.

✦ ✦ ✦

The Best Question

"How can I fail?" This is the question that you should be asking yourself when you first begin working with your goals. Questions like these will put your mind in motion, and will keep your attitude positive even in the face of minor setbacks.

✦ ✦ ✦

Where Did the Time Go?

A few days without giving thought to your goals can easily become a few weeks and months. Don't let too much time go by without giving thought to your objectives. If you don't write it down, talk about it, and think about it during your daily activities, your goal stands a small chance of success.

✦ ✦ ✦

Take a Break

Although you don't want to go too far without working on your to-do lists, taking a break is not only acceptable, it's recommended. Working too long without a break can take its toll on your body and mind, lowering your effectiveness and creativity. Take a break ev-

If it was an overnight success, it was one long, hard, sleepless night.

Dicky Barrett

Measure with Your Computer

A fast and easy way to measure your progress is to use your home computer. Programs like Microsoft Excel™ have charts and formula functions that will make your record keeping a breeze.

ery now and then to relax, refresh, and reflect. The length of your break can be as little as five minutes to as long as a weekend.

✦ ✦ ✦

Think Outside the Box

Don't be trapped by comfortable and conventional thinking. If an idea will help you reach your goal, do it. Be crazy, wacky, and outrageous. If wearing a shirt that says, "Ask me about my goals!" helps keep you motivated, wear the shirt.

✦ ✦ ✦

Mix the Categories

After brainstorming, you will create goals from many different areas of your life. Choose one goal from each category. For example, if you have three health goals, two career goals, and two financial goals, try working on one goal from each group. This will keep you from being overwhelmed with any one category.

✦ ✦ ✦

If You Miss the Target, Change Your Aim

A goal that is giving you trouble is not something out of the ordinary. Goal reaching, by definition, is not easy work. Giving up at the first sign of trouble isn't an option. However, if you find that the goal you have chosen simply isn't working at the time, choose another goal from your list to replace it. This way you will still be improving in that particular area of your life.

✦ ✦ ✦

Starting Off Right

You wake up in the morning, reach for the towel, and head off to the shower. The next step you take is of the utmost importance. To think, or not to think. I suggest the former. Use the time in the shower to go over your goals for the day, to think of new angles to take with them, and new goals that you may want to work towards.

✦ ✦ ✦

What's the Temp?

Do you remember the posters with a thermometer on them? The ones that tracked an organization's progress towards their goal? If so, use it! If not, simply draw a large thermometer on a sheet of blank paper. Along the side, write in each level of your goal. As you reach those levels, color the area at and below the line. Soon you'll find that your thermometer is filled to the top. Success!

Go for the moon. If you don't get it, you'll still be heading for a star.

Willis Reed

13

Reminders

LIFE MOVES FAST and that is why you need to take steps to ensure that your goals won't get lost in the shuffle. With all of your responsibilities and jobs to look after, it is easy to see how your longer-term objectives can be put aside for more immediate issues. Even with a hectic schedule it is easy to keep your goals alive and well.

The next chapter will show you how to use simple tips and techniques to keep you reminded of, and working towards, the goals you've created. You've put in the time and effort to create effective goals, and you owe it to yourself to see them to the end.

Places to Post

Be creative with your reminders. After you write your goal out on a sheet of paper, try these ideas:
- ✧ in your closet
- ✧ bathroom mirror
- ✧ on your visor in the car
- ✧ below the television

Your Calendar and a Red Marker

Place a large circle around the day you want to reach your goal with a red marker. This is a quick and easy way to be reminded of your goal daily. If your calendar is hanging in a high traffic area you will constantly see your deadline. Now that's motivation.

✦ ✦ ✦

Computer Calendar Program

Many of today's computers come with some type of calendar program pre-installed. Type an 'x' on your deadline and print out the calendar month. Make copies and place them around the house or office.

✦ ✦ ✦

Carry a Mini-Calendar

Not everyone has a calendar around constantly. This makes it hard to see your goal on a daily basis. The solution is to purchase a smaller, pocket-sized calendar. You will be able to check through your goals and task lists daily without having a large calendar to lug around.

✦ ✦ ✦

Cut Out Deadline

If you have a calendar that isn't in use, or if you wish to purchase a second one, cut out your deadline and keep the small square close to you. Your wallet or purse is a great place to keep your reminder.

✦ ✦ ✦

Calendars Everywhere!

Calendars are relatively inexpensive and the number of different styles and types are in the thousands. Put a calendar in your room, home office, kitchen, den, office, car, etc. The more often you can see your deadline, the more motivation you will have to work towards your goal.

✦ ✦ ✦

Don't Forget About Mini-Goals

Use your calendar to mark down the deadlines of sub and mini-goals. These deadlines are just as important as the ultimate objective. You will also have daily or weekly motivation to keep going. If you only wrote the deadline of your main goal, you may feel overwhelmed by how far away, or how close, it is. By listing sub-goals in your planner you will maintain constant motivation.

✦ ✦ ✦

Purchase a Planner

A personal planner is a great investment. From the most basic to the most complex, you can easily find a planner to fit your needs. This tool will not only help you keep your schedule organized and efficient, but will also make for easier goal achievement and motivation.

✦ ✦ ✦

Mark Your Planner

Turn to the deadline of your goal in your planner, take a red felt-tip pen, and write your goal in bold letters. Make it a point each day to turn to that page and read your goal. For many people, their planner is what keeps them going through the day. Putting a goal in that frequently viewed planner will almost guarantee motivation.

> *Time flies like an arrow. Fruit flies like a banana.*
>
> Lisa Grossman

Set Your Watch

Set your watch alarm to remind you to work on your goals. If you want to work out at six o'clock at night, set your watch and put your mind at ease.

Page Number One

Take a page in your planner that is slated for notes and make it your first page when you open your planner. Write your goal, or several goals, on that page. From now on you'll see your goal every time you open your planner. This solves the problem of having a goal that is outside of the current month. For example, if it is October and you have a major goal in August you may never see that deadline until Summer. With a simple readjustment of pages you'll fix this problem.

✦ ✦ ✦

Print It, Tape It Up, Achieve It

Using your basic word processing program, type your goal in bold letters. Print it out, make several copies, and tape your goal up as a reminder. The idea is to keep your goals safe from the daily clutter and hectic pace. Many times our goals have to take a back seat to problems that demand our attention. Keeping your goal visible will help you make it a reality.

✦ ✦ ✦

A Bookmark Reminder

Use your bookmark as a goal reminder. If you read often you will be able to see your goal before and after you read your book. This tip is even more useful when reading a book that motivates you. For instance, if you are reading a book about overcoming the most challenging odds, and your goal is to quit smoking, you will read your goal and feel inspired to succeed.

✦ ✦ ✦

Tape Yourself, Replay

Tape yourself stating your goal. Replay the tape when you need motivation or revitalization. You can even take it a step further and talk about why you want this goal. Explain what first inspired you to take on the goal, and the plan you have for reaching it. This simple tip will help you create your own motivational audiotape.

❖ ❖ ❖

You may delay, but time will not.

Benjamin Franklin

Use People as a Reminder

When you share your goals with friends and family, let them know that reminding you about your objectives, or asking you about your progress is more than welcome. Other people are really good at asking you about your personal business. You can use these encounters as reminders and motivation. As your friends ask about the progress, you can take that opportunity to talk about what you've achieved, how you will proceed, and how happy you'll be when finished.

❖ ❖ ❖

Crazy? Yes, But It Worked!

An associate of mind once taught his bird to say, "Climb the mountain!" His goal was to climb Grand Mt. Monadnock. Having that goal repeated to him every day kept his mind focused on his primary aim.

❖ ❖ ❖

Team Up With a Holiday

If your deadline is near a holiday, link them together. For example, if you want to save $1,000 by January, 2005, use New Year's Day

Tag Along

Associate your goal with things that you see often. This will ensure that your goal stays in front of you in the mix of your daily responsibilities and duties. The following examples will help you get started. Try associating:

◇ the pleasant receptionist with being positive

◇ the clock with being more efficient at work

◇ a pair of shoes with working out and running

as the deadline. This is an easy way to keep the goal at the top of your mind. Commercials, ads in magazines, and other people will be constantly mentioning or referring to that holiday. Now you'll even have motivation from the media.

✦ ✦ ✦

Tie a Ribbon Around a Tree

Use a ribbon as a reminder. Tie it around your doorknob to remind you to think positively at work. Tie a ribbon around your purse to remind you to save money at the store. You can even tie a ribbon around your computer to remind you to work on your home business.

✦ ✦ ✦

Use a Ring as a Reminder

If you wear rings, use one as a symbol for what you are trying to achieve. This is a great way to remind you on a daily basis of what you are working towards. You can use different rings to represent different areas of your life. Just make sure you don't overdo it and wear more jewelry than your hands can hold.

✦ ✦ ✦

Purchase a Bulletin Board

Aside from leaving messages and posting notes, a bulletin board is a great way to remind you about your goals. Write your goal on a small piece of paper and place it in a corner of the board. Each time you look at your bulletin board you will see your target.

✦ ✦ ✦

Put a Dry Erase Board in Your Home & Office

This is one of the best investments you can make. Purchasing a small dry-erase board is an excellent and low-cost method of motivation. Write the plan for your goal on the board, cross steps out as you finish them, and write additional notes or steps as you go along.

✦ ✦ ✦

Split Boards in Half

Whether you have a bulletin board or a dry-erase board, split it in half with a marker line or a thin piece of construction paper. One side is for short-term goals and the other will be for long-term objectives. This will keep both short and long-term targets at the front of your mind.

✦ ✦ ✦

Display the Finished Product

If you are writing a book, put a book by your work station. Keeping a tangible representation of your goal clearly in sight will keep you reminded and motivated. It will help you to realize that you can do it because others have done it.

If you don't know where you are going, you will probably end up somewhere else.

Lawrence J. Peter

14

Goals at Work

A N IMPORTANT PART OF GOAL SETTING and accomplishment happens at work. Using goals at work will help you to produce greater results and stay motivated, which will add to job satisfaction and fulfillment. When you bring your goal skills to the job you'll also be making life better for your co-workers and boss.

You need to enjoy your work and feel like you are reaching your full potential in your career. Goals offer a very important step towards that end. Use the tips that follow and share them with others who wish to succeed in the workplace.

Record Setters

Healthy competition can be very motivating. Find out from others or through available resources what records have been set within your organization. Perhaps an old employee set a sales record three years ago. It will give you new goals and enthusiasm.

Communicate Your Goals to Management

After creating your work goals, share them with management to make sure they are aware of the direction you are taking. You wouldn't want to put your heart and soul into a project that management will eliminate.

✦ ✦ ✦

Fax Your Goals to Work

Want to keep your goals with you at work? Have you thought of a great idea at home and want to make sure it gets to the office? Fax it! This is a great way to keep motivated at work and to have your job goals sent to you quickly and easily.

✦ ✦ ✦

Use Notes

Write short reminders on a notepad and place them on your computer screen or desk. Just don't overdo it. You want to be able to actually see your desk in the morning. Sometimes a quick reminder is all you need to make for an effective and motivated workday.

✦ ✦ ✦

Have a Work Notebook Handy

When talking with the boss or working with your peers, have a notebook handy to write down goals and tasks that need to be done. Our memories are amazing but without training they can have a difficult time retrieving every fact and idea that we hear in one day. With your notes in writing, you'll be certain to keep goals and tasks at work clear and readily available.

Look to the Competition

If you are having trouble thinking of the right goals to work for, look to see what your competition is doing. This will give you several ideas to work with.

✦ ✦ ✦

The Company Goals

Have a meeting with your immediate boss and discuss the goals of the company. After interpreting this information you will be able to create goals that work with, and not against, your companies objectives. Conflicting goals will cause many problems internally and externally. Steer clear of these problems and talk about goals first.

✦ ✦ ✦

Have a Plan of Action Before You Begin

Time is the greatest resource we have, so you don't want to waste any of it when you get to work. Have a plan of action before you enter the doors. This way you'll be able to go to work immediately and get the most done in the shortest amount of time.

✦ ✦ ✦

At the End of the Day

Before you leave each day write up a plan for tomorrow. With the current jobs fresh in your mind you will be able to make an effective outline of the next day's to-do list.

If opportunity doesn't knock, build a door.

Milton Berle

15

Children & Goals

THE VALUE OF GOALS needs to be taught to children. It has been shown that teaching children lessons at an early age makes a greater impact than waiting until they are older. Knowing that you need to open your child's eyes to the power of goals is one thing, but how do you go about doing it?

That is the goal of this chapter. This group of tips and ideas will help you to help your kids. Some are simple tricks to help you introduce goals into their lives while others pose more thought-provoking challenges. After using these tips with your kids you'll be amazed at how much the understanding of goals can do for your family.

Emphasize Intrinsic Rewards

If the goal is something that they want, don't offer them external rewards. This will only serve to decrease their internal motivation. Instead, remind them of the intrinsic rewards they will receive by reaching their goals. Remember to talk in terms that your children will understand. Several internal rewards include:

❖ increased confidence
❖ pride in their work and abilities
❖ personal growth
❖ improved self-esteem

Explain the Importance of Goals

Teach your children about the benefits of setting a goal and working towards it. You don't want to overdo it, but getting the general idea into their heads will help them in their lives. The goal process symbolizes hard work, dedication, commitment, creativity, cooperation, learning, failing, succeeding, and growing. These are lessons that every child should learn.

✦ ✦ ✦

Make It Fun

When working with your kids, you have to make the idea of goals fun. Explain how exciting it is to reach a goal, how much more fun life is when you use them, and how they can do it too. Keep it interesting and fun, and they are sure to catch onto the idea.

✦ ✦ ✦

Set Goals with School

An excellent area for your children to start using goals is at school. You should let them set their own personal goals. Test scores, homework grades, or attendance are a few areas that could be integrated with goals. Be sure to keep it positive and upbeat.

✦ ✦ ✦

Lead by Example

If you talk about the importance of goals but do not have any yourself, your words will have little impact. You must talk about the goals you have, explain why they are important to you, and celebrate your accomplishments with the whole family.

✦ ✦ ✦

Help Them Set Goals

Located in this book are hundreds of tips about setting effective and efficient goals. Use these tips and other ideas that you have discovered to help your children set smart goals.

✦ ✦ ✦

It Must Be Their Goal

Your children's goals must be your children's goals. For example, if you have a goal for your children to win first place at a swimming meet, that doesn't necessarily mean that they will share your view. Pushing goals onto your children will not only decrease their motivation and enjoyment, but it will also diminish their desire to use goals in the future. You can help in the process as long as the overall goal is theirs.

✦ ✦ ✦

Have a Special Goal Night

If you want to teach your children an important aspect of success and achievement, have a weekly or monthly night when the topic of talk is goals. This will teach them that you must stay on top of your dreams, and that a goal will only come to fruition if it is constantly attended.

✦ ✦ ✦

Let Them Teach You

After your kids have set a few goals for themselves, let them explain their system. This isn't a time for you to be critical, it is a time for you to let your children shine and enjoy the experience of teaching you something they have created.

It is never too late to be who you might have been.

George Eliot

Do You Need Help?

Ask your children for help with your goals. It will make them feel important and more mature. They may surprise you with some great ideas.

Smart Rewards

When a child reaches a goal, give them a smart reward. Money, candy, video games, and the like are not smart rewards. They will put too much attention towards the wrong ends. The greatest reward, as you know, is reaching the goal itself. If you can relay that message to your children, then you will be doing them a greater service than any tip or idea can offer within these pages.

✦ ✦ ✦

Praise

The two keys here are consistency and sincerity. Praise that comes for a good grade for one child and not the other will not only confuse the system, but also hurt the child and his or her view of hard work. When you praise your kids, you must also praise sincerely. Kids, as well as adults, are adept at recognizing a real compliment as opposed to an insincere one. Make sure your praise is equal and comes from the heart.

✦ ✦ ✦

Share Your Successes

Share your goals and success stories with your kids. This will not only be leading by example but also proving that it really works. If you have childhood examples of goal setting and achievement, all the better. Your children will relate to stories about kids and goals.

✦ ✦ ✦

Ask Them About Their Goals

They have spent a lot of thought and time on their goals, and that in itself deserves recog-

nition. Ask them about their goals, their progress, and if they need any help along the way. This is the most effective and important reward; attention. More than anything else, children crave attention and recognition. Asking your kids about their dreams, hopes, goals, and ambitions will be giving them the greatest motivation of all.

❖ ❖ ❖

Failing is Okay

This is a lesson for both children and adults to take to heart. Too often we give up at the first sign of failure when success is only a short distance away. Everyone, from Olympic athletes to world-renowned scientists, has failed more times than they have succeeded. It is a fact of life. It wouldn't be natural to get everything right the first time. Everyone agrees, but few keep trying after the first failure. We must learn from our mistakes, improve accordingly, and move on.

❖ ❖ ❖

Create Games to Teach

Goal setting is an excellent tool for anyone to have. When it is transferred to children, it must be done delicately. Make a game out of the whole idea. Challenge them to solve simple problems using goals. Have them create simple charts to measure their progress, or have a wish-list game.

❖ ❖ ❖

Start Small

An important tip to remember when helping your children understand the power of goal setting is to keep it simple. Although they

There are no shortcuts to any place worth going.

Beverly Sills

Hold them Accountable

When a deadline shows up for one of your children's goals, check to see if they have accomplished their task. This will teach them that they will be held accountable for their actions and that you care about their success. If a deadline is allowed to be ignored, they may learn that following through on jobs isn't important.

are young and inexperienced, the lessons of hard work and dedication should be shared with everyone. Start small and build as time goes on.

16

The Plan

THERE ARE MANY DIFFERENT WAYS to categorize goals. I have chosen to break them up into personal, health, career, relationship, and financial goals. These goals cover the majority of issues you will be facing throughout your life. Each category is important to the overall picture and is much like the building blocks of motivation; if one is missing the entire system falls apart.

Use a sheet of paper, your personal computer, or the lines provided to answer each of the questions in this chapter. After doing so, you will have a great plan to start with. As time goes on you can add additional questions or factors to make your plan of action more customized and consistent with your needs.

PERSONAL GOALS

Wishes and Dreams

Make a list of your long-term goals for personal achievement.

_____

_____

Life Improvements

Make a list of personal improvements you would like make. These include changes in your personality, attitude, or overall character.

_____

_____

Toleration

Make a list of the situations or circumstances that you are tolerating in your life, but would be happier if they were resolved or improved.

_____

_____

Hobbies

Make a list of the hobbies you would like to become involved with.

_____

_____

Travel

Make a list of the places you would like to visit sometime in your life.

_____

_____

Languages

Are there any languages that you are interested in learning?

Areas of Interest

What interests you? What sparks your curiosity? List as many ideas as you can think of.

Musical Instruments

What musical instruments have you been interested in learning how to play?

Habits to Drop

What habits do you have that you would like to eliminate?

Habits to Gain

What positive habits would you like to gain?

Ambitions

What are you ambitions? What lofty goals do you have?

Easy Goals

Make a list of smaller goals that will easily be accomplished with some time and effort. These are important to build confidence and start you in the right direction.

FINANCIAL GOALS

Savings - Current Status

What amount do you currently have in your savings account? What portion of your salary do you put away each month? What other sources of income do you have that contribute to your savings account?

Savings - Goals

How much money would you like to have in your savings account in one year? Five years? Ten years? How much would you like to be able to put away each month?

Savings - Plan

Considering where you are now, and where you want to be, how much money will you need to increase your monthly amount by? What steps could you take to increase the amount of savings or decrease your expenses?

_____

_____

Checking - Current Status

What do you currently have in your checking account? What do you designate your checking account for? Bills? Mortgage? Groceries?

_____

_____

Checking - Goals

Total your monthly expenses to find out how much you will need to put into your checking account. It may be a good idea to put in more than you will need for a safety net. What would you like to have in your checking account each month to cover your living expenses?

_____

_____

Checking - Plan

Using your current situation and goals, how much of an increase is needed? What steps can you take to make this work?

_____

_____

Salary - Current Status

How much do you make at your job? Including other resources of income, what is your monthly total?

_____

_____

Salary - Goal

How much money would you like to make?

_____

_____

Salary - Plan

Increasing your salary isn't always about getting a raise or a new job. You can also offer to start new projects or ventures and ask for a percentage of the profits. Make a thorough list of the different ways to increase your salary.

_____

_____

College Fund

If you have children, or are planning on having them, do you want to set up a college fund? If so, you will need to start growing a college fund now or in the near future. With the rising costs of tuition at many colleges throughout the U.S., you will need a hefty sum by the time they are ready for post high school education.

_____

_____

Retirement Savings

This is perhaps the most important financial plan to consider. The cost of retiring comfortably is not a small figure, and therefore you must create a plan early on to ensure a smooth transition from the working world into retirement. Remember to take inflation into account when you create your plan.

Vacation

If you are a frequent vacationer, plan your yearly budget accordingly. Take the average cost of your trip multiplied by the average number of trips per year.

Unexpected Expenses

Choose an amount to cover unexpected expenses. This number will vary according to lifestyle, family size and characteristics, etc.

Spending

Keep track of your monthly spending. This includes grocery shopping, miscellaneous purchases, and other smaller areas of spending.

Investments

Invest in your future. If you haven't already done so, meet with a financial advisor and set up an investment portfolio that matches your needs. Include in your financial plan the amount you would like to invest.

Financial Plans

Write out a five, ten, and twenty-year plan for your finances. Include desired income, savings, and investment capital.

If You Miss the Mark

If you set a savings goal of $100 per week, but only put in $90.00, make up for the difference in your next deposit. That way you can stick to the original plan.

✦ ✦ ✦

Teach Your Children Well

The importance of saving and investing in your future is something your older children could prosper from. Planning for tomorrow is a necessity for the happy, healthy, and successful person.

CAREER GOALS

Where are You Now?

Write down characteristics of your current job. Write down what you do on an average day and what the future holds if you continue on this path.

Where Do You Want to Be?

If you don't know where you want to be in five years, you will most likely end up somewhere you probably wouldn't have chosen. Make a plan for your career in five, ten, and twenty year increments. Write down the position you will have, the salary that comes with it, and the education you will receive from it.

What Do You Like?

Write down a list of things you enjoy at your current job. This includes individual duties all the way to general responsibilities and functions.

What's Missing?

Make a list of the things that you don't like about your current job. What aspects are missing that would make things better?

Your Timeline

Create a timeline of action. When do you want to start looking for a new job or begin work to improve your current job? Where do you want to end up at retirement?

Are You On the Right Path?

Ask yourself, "Am I heading in the right direction?" If not, then a change must be made if you wish to succeed.

Passion

What do you love doing? Try to include that hobby or pastime in your five, ten, and twenty year plans.

Get the Details

When you know the position you would like to have, get all of the information you can about that job. Knowing the specifics of a particular job increases your chances of actually making it all come into place. Make phone calls, visit the library, look online, and get in touch with the companies that offer your desired career position. As you learn of the specifics, list them on a sheet of paper to build a detailed position description.

Goals to Get There

After you know what is required in your field, use your goal setting skills to create a plan of action to get there.

Keep Your Eyes Open

Keep alert to job openings in your desired field. Check papers, look at online job sites, and contact potential organizations about their openings. Make a list of the openings and opportunities you see.

Join the Appropriate Clubs and Organizations

If you want to be a public speaker, join a Toastmasters club or the National Speakers Association. If you wish to a be a writer, join a writer's guild or writing workshop. Whatever you want to become, join the clubs and organizations that will help you to make your career dream a reality. What clubs and groups offer support for your field?

Create a Resume

If you haven't already done so, create a professional and updated resume.

✦ ✦ ✦

Talk About It

If you have decided to make a career change, tell your friends about it, and let them know that they should keep you updated of news they hear about potential openings.

✦ ✦ ✦

Why You Should Share

Sharing your career goals not only gives you a new set of eyes and ears, but it also increases your dedication to the idea. If you talk about it on a daily basis, you start to really get used to the idea and your motivation increases every time it comes up in conversation.

✦ ✦ ✦

RELATIONSHIP GOALS

Family

What type of relationship do you wish to have with each of your family members? What steps need to be taken to make that happen?

Friendships

What type of relationship do you wish to have with each one of your friends? What steps need to be taken in order for you to have these types of relationships?

Personal

What type of person do you want to be? What characteristics would you like to have? Make a list of the character traits you like and those that you would like to change.

The Reasons Why

If you find that things are not going as they should be, find the source of the problem and work to fix it. Relationship goals are not numbers or statistics, and must be treated differently than financial or health goals. A softer approach is necessary, but an approach is needed just the same. Leaving your relationships to chance is just as unhealthy as leaving your finances or career to chance.

HEALTH GOALS

Vital Signs - Current Status

Write down your current weight, height, blood pressure and cholesterol. You will have to get a check-up for the latter two numbers.

_____

_____

Vital Signs - Goals

Where do you want your weight, blood pressure, and cholesterol? Be sure to ask your doctor what levels are healthy for your body type and age.

_____

_____

Vital Signs - Plan

What steps do you need to take in order for your blood pressure, cholesterol, and weight, if necessary, to come down? What lifestyle changes should be made?

_____

_____

Diet - Current Status

Keep track of what you eat for an entire week. Create a simple chart listing the days of the week on one side and meals on the other.

_____

_____

Diet - Goals

Based on the weight, blood pressure, cholesterol, and energy levels you wish to maintain, what type of diet is necessary? This may take some research, but where your health is concerned, the time is well spent.

Diet - Plan

After researching what types of foods are necessary for healthy living, make out a grocery list that includes these items. Keep track of what you eat for a week to ensure that your new diet is taking hold and improving your lifestyle.

Sleep - Current Status

How much sleep you do normally get per night?

Sleep - Goals

What amount of sleep is required for you to realize your desired energy and stress levels?

Sleep - Plan

What steps do you need to take in order to get enough sleep? Write down changes you will make in your daily schedule so you can stick with the plan.

_____

_____

Exercise - Current Status

How often do you exercise? What types of exercising do you currently do?

_____

_____

Exercise - Goals

This is one of the most important aspects of a healthy lifestyle. What exercise programs are recommended to meet your personal goals?

_____

_____

Exercise - Plan

Create an exercise program that takes into account your current situation and where you want to be. Write down how often you will exercise, with whom, and where it will take place. If you plan to join a health club, write down the contact information.

_____

_____

Stress - Current Status

Make a list of the things that stress you out. What would you gauge your average stress level to be? Low? Medium? High?

Stress - Goals

Write down how you would like to deal with stress. For example, you could write down that you will not get stressed when someone complains about their day to you.

Stress - Plan

Write out how you will meet your stress goals. What steps do you need to take in order to lower your stress? Do you need to create stress-reducing habits such as counting to ten or taking a five minute break throughout the day? Write down your plan of action to lower stress.

SECTION THREE
Attitude

17

The Power of a Positive Attitude

A POSITIVE ATTITUDE can change your future. It can open your eyes to opportunity and improve your mental and physical health. A positive attitude can also improve your relationships with your friends and family. These are only a few of the many benefits of a positive attitude. Knowing these ideas will serve to motivate you to make improvements in your outlook on life.

This chapter will help you to realize why anyone would want a positive attitude. After you understand what the right attitude can do for you, it will be easier for you to make improvements that last.

You're Not in a Bubble

The power of attitude, both negative and positive, is not isolated. When you have a positive attitude it rubs off on others around you. The same is true of a negative outlook on things. You will be affecting:

✧ family members
✧ friends
✧ co-workers
✧ strangers

The Ultimate Good

You will be able to look at the world with a new set of eyes. Your attitude doesn't only come into play with winning and losing or dealing with negative situations, it encompasses everything in your life. It includes how you treat other people, plan for your future, and deal with daily living. When you improve your attitude, you will be improving every aspect of your life.

✦ ✦ ✦

Dealing with Failure

With a positive attitude you will handle failure for what it is; a temporary setback. A negative attitude sees failing as the end of the line. If at first you don't succeed, go do something else. When you have a positive attitude you can see that failing is useful and necessary for a successful and happy life. You will be able to fail and then try again.

✦ ✦ ✦

A Friendlier Personality

People, for the most part, enjoy a positive person's company. When you have a positive attitude, people will gravitate towards you. When things aren't going well for others, you'll find that they like to be around you simply because of your positive attitude. Your good mood will rub off on them.

✦ ✦ ✦

Bucking for Promotion

You will enjoy more success at work. Studies have shown that one of the main reasons you get a job, keep a job, and get promoted within the company is influenced by your attitude. Not only will you enjoy better relationships but you will also enjoy a more satisfying career.

✦ ✦ ✦

Family Life

You will improve your family life. As your attitude improves, so too will the relationships you have with your family. You spend your greatest amount of time with them and your true attitude is expressed more in the home than anywhere else. A confident and positive attitude will create a happy, friendly environment for your children and spouse.

There are no menial jobs, only menial attitudes.

William Bennett

✦ ✦ ✦

Changing Your Environment

You will be able to improve negative situations. When you enter into a negative environment or conversation, your attitude will affect those around you. People feed off the moods and attitudes of other people. When you bring a positive outlook to situations, you can take a negative and leave it as a positive. The power of your attitude will improve the situation and the attitudes of those that come into contact with you.

✦ ✦ ✦

Success

You will be, without a doubt, more successful. The reason lies in how you perceive problems. When a problem arises, as one most certainly will nearly every day, a person with a negative attitude responds with anger, frustration and surrender. "It just won't work." When a person with a positive attitude con-

Living Longer

The health benefits of having a positive attitude are obvious: less stress, worry, anger, frustration, etc. This will in turn help you live a longer, healthier life. Not only will it make each day better, but it will give you more days to enjoy.

fronts a problem, it's a completely different story. The first thing you do is take a logical look at the situation. After some thought you create several solutions and scenarios for action. You choose the best one, implement it and your seemingly impossible situation is transformed into an opportunity. With a positive attitude you will see through the problems and look for the answers. It sounds so simple and yet this type of thinking is rare. For you, it will be typical.

✦ ✦ ✦

Mr. or Mrs. Answer

People will begin to look to you for help and advice. This will go a long way in building your confidence. You will be given more respect as people look to you for direction and support.

✦ ✦ ✦

Worry, Stress, and Anger

As your attitude shifts, your propensity towards worry, stress, and anger will decline. This happens because you will be able to deal with stressful situations with relative ease. When you can see the solution in a problem, you won't go through the hair-pulling frustration that so many people deal with.

✦ ✦ ✦

Health Improvements

Your health will improve. Stress and tension are deadly. They cause more problems in your life than you may think. A positive attitude decreases stress and that in turn decreases the damage it can do to your body. Less stress, better health.

✦ ✦ ✦

Negative Pushes - Positive Pulls

The saddest thing about a negative attitude is its effect on personal relationships. As time goes on, most negative people will push their friends away because of their bad moods and abrasive personalities. People don't especially enjoy being around a pessimist, and that will begin to show. A positive attitude pulls people towards you.

◆ ◆ ◆

Making Matters Worse

A negative attitude can take a neutral situation and make it worse. For example, if a person walks into work with a bad attitude, their negativity can flow to co-workers. Soon you could have a whole group of crabby workers when only moments ago everyone was pleasant.

◆ ◆ ◆

A Boost in Confidence

Your confidence will improve. When you turn problems into solutions, gain respect from your peers, and make situations better simply because of your presence, you will begin to feel a lot better about yourself. Confidence is a necessary trait for happiness, and with your new attitude you'll have more than enough of it.

◆ ◆ ◆

Laughter

It's been credited for being the best medicine, and I couldn't agree more. When your attitude is positive, you'll find that you laugh a lot more. Hopefully you'll find yourself smiling when you think about your life and what lies ahead.

Two men look out the same prison bars; one sees mud and the other stars.

Frederick Langbridge

Quick Turnaround

When you are in the middle of a bad situation you will be able to turn your mood around quickly. This skill is very important in the business world and at home where you don't always have the luxury of being upset for a prolonged period of time.

Education and Curiosity

Individuals with positive attitudes have been shown to educate themselves more than those with negative or neutral attitudes. One of the keys to motivation, success, and happiness in life is continuous education and improvement.

18

Improving Your Attitude

THIS IS ONE OF THE MOST important parts of motivation. It takes the right attitude to get motivated about changing your life for the better. It takes the right attitude to fail, get back up, brush off the dirt and try again. Only with a positive attitude can you make long-lasting improvements and successes a reality.

Your attitude, as you will soon find out, is completely in your control. People can try to change it and affect it, but only you give the final okay. The ideas you are about to learn will show you how to take control, create the attitude you want to have, and make it last.

Everyone You Meet You

can learn something from everyone you meet. Their experiences, skills, and viewpoints will be different from yours. This gives you the opportunity to learn something new from each person you meet.

When It's Time to Change

If you find that you look at things negatively, or would like to be happier, decide to change. That's where it all starts. It could even be today, after reading this tip. Before you can really make improvements you have to be committed to the challenge.

✦ ✦ ✦

Your Daily Moods

You become your daily moods. Statements like, "I'm only crabby in the mornings," or, "I only get like this a few times a week," could be indicators of a growing problem. Don't let a string of bad moods become your overall attitude. When you feel like things haven't been going well for several days, do something about it. Before you know it, a few bad days can create the image that you are usually an unhappy person. You may think bad moods here and there are acceptable, until you realize that they have consumed the greater part of your time. The good news is that small steps, taken consistently, can make huge improvements in your attitude.

✦ ✦ ✦

A Reflection of Our Moods

For an indication of your mood, look to see how other people treat you. We may not want to admit being upset to ourselves, but until we accept the truth about our attitude we cannot improve it. Look to see how people treat you, listen to you, and respond to you. Learn about yourself by watching and listening to others.

✦ ✦ ✦

Being Honest

If you aren't in a good mood, or have had a string of bad days, admit it. Unfortunately, or fortunately depending on how you look at it, other people are reluctant to let us know that we are being negative or moody. They may think it to themselves but they aren't going to share that information with you. Because of this, it's most often up to you to take account of your moods. Part of the process of overcoming negativity is accepting your current state before you try changing it.

Ability is what you're capable of doing. Motivation determines what you do. Attitude determines how well you do it.

Lou Holtz

✦ ✦ ✦

Does Your Mood Shift on a Regular Basis?

If you cannot target specific events that affect your mood or attitude negatively, you may find that your mood is more like a roller coaster, hitting peaks and valleys throughout the day. This is nothing to be worried about. The tips within this book are geared towards both event specific and non-event specific attitude improvement. Knowing what area you are trying to improve makes the diagnosis of helpful tips and ideas a more exact science.

✦ ✦ ✦

The Mirror

Look in the mirror in the morning or at night to get a good glimpse of what others see. Your attitude is greatly affected by those around you. Because of this, it's important to understand how you are affecting other people. You may feel fine inside, but if your face tells a different story, you're not communicating it well.

I Can Beat That!

Avoid the bad news game with others. It's the game that starts with, "My back aches," and you respond, "Well, I've had a head-ache for nine days," and they come back with, "Both my arms are broken." You don't have to prove that things are worse on your end. Be happy that they aren't and move on.

Testing, Testing

Test your ideas. Examine the results from your techniques. You don't have to go so far as to take attitude tests before and after. This tip simply means to take note of how ideas work out for you. If you find that one tip helps es-pecially well, don't forget it.

✦ ✦ ✦

How Do You Normally Respond?

When a stressful situation occurs, how do you normally respond? Do they leave you feeling uneasy, uncomfortable or tense? Write down a list of common responses to difficult situa-tions. Once you know how you react you'll be able to focus on finding specific solutions for your attitude instead of vague ideas.

✦ ✦ ✦

How'd They Do That?

Ask others around you how they maintain positive attitudes. They may have some great tips or tricks that work really well, but you won't know about them until you ask. When you become curious about how things work, you'll be overwhelmed with solutions, answers, and ideas to help you improve your life.

✦ ✦ ✦

Anything Goes

Be creative. That's one way to ensure that you not only find ways to make things better, but you'll have fun while you're doing it. Who cares how crazy the idea sounds at first, give it a try. The answer may lie in the most un-common techniques.

✦ ✦ ✦

It Takes Effort

Almost everything that is worthwhile takes hard work and dedicated effort. Improving your attitude is no different. It will take time to make changes in your life. You must be willing to put in the effort required to create long-lasting improvements. If you do, then you get what you want.

✦ ✦ ✦

What Do Your Friends Think?

Ask your friends and family what they think about your attitude. You may be surprised to find that it doesn't exactly match what you had in mind. If it doesn't, don't take it personally. They are simply trying to help you out. Take their constructive criticism for what it is, constructive. If you are willing to take opinions from others about your attitude, then you are definitely on the road to an improved outlook.

✦ ✦ ✦

Become a Student of Attitude

Watch others around you. How do they react to situations? Would you respond the same way? Things are always different when you see someone else doing it. You may realize that something you do doesn't seem as logical when someone else is doing it. It's all about finding the attitude for you, the one that you feel is right and worth working toward.

✦ ✦ ✦

Discover Your Own Personal Buttons

We all have buttons. They are either our 'good' buttons, or the other kind. Knowing both is important. Learn about your buttons and how

The optimist sees opportunity in every danger; the pessimist sees danger in every opportunity.

Winston Churchill

Remember the Time

When you are in the middle of a great moment, take something tangible away from it to serve as a pleasant reminder of the time. If you had a great time with your family at the beach, bring home a shell or rock. When you need a little boost you can look to your symbol to remind you of great memories.

you can use them to your advantage. If you are in a bad mood, take steps to improve it by pushing your 'good' buttons. For example, if you know that reading calms your nerves, have a book handy for stressful situations.

✦ ✦ ✦

Pessimism is Not a Choice

Many people think having a negative attitude is just another way of looking at life, or being 'realistic'. I couldn't disagree more. When the choice between being positive and negative receives equal praise, we are looking at the picture all wrong. Being negative is something you should want to change. Being positive is something you should strive to become. One is not an equal to the other. One is the valley, while the other is the peak.

✦ ✦ ✦

You Can Change

The most important thing to remember about your attitude is that it can be changed. "That's the way I am, and that's how I will always be," doesn't hold up to what I have personally experienced and seen in other people. You can change every aspect of who you are for better or worse.

✦ ✦ ✦

The Root of the Worry

An unrealized goal could be causing subconscious negativity towards non-related areas of your life. For example, if you have continued to smoke after trying to quit for years, that stress and frustration could carry over into other areas of your life. It is important to find the source of your attitude problems. You may be trying to find solutions to a cause that isn't responsible for your ultimate attitude.

✦ ✦ ✦

What Are You Missing?

Make a list of things that you desire in your life, but have yet to attain. This may bring to your attention the real reasons for negativity or moodiness.

✦ ✦ ✦

Laugh

Laugh at yourself. Laugh with others. Laugh out loud. Laugh to yourself. Laugh when you watch movies. Laugh when you watch television shows. Laugh when you hear jokes. Laugh when you tell jokes, but only if they're funny. Laugh in the morning. Laugh in the afternoon. Laugh in the evening. Laughter is the best medicine for your physical, mental, and emotional health.

✦ ✦ ✦

Put Things in Perspective

No matter how bad you think you have it, someone, somewhere, has it worse. It's not a happy thought, but it can help to put your problems in perspective. Remember to look at the big picture when it comes to your problems. You will still need to deal with them, but your attitude towards these problems will be positive and you will have a greater amount of understanding.

✦ ✦ ✦

Your Home Environment

Get organized at home. To maintain that winning attitude from work to home you must

Nothing can stop the man with the right mental attitude from achieving his goal; nothing on earth can help the man with the wrong mental attitude.

Thomas Jefferson

Your Work Environment

Get organized at work. Working in a clean and organized environment is not only necessary for a motivated mind, but also for a positive attitude. Take time to clean your desk, files, and computer files. Keep only the items that you will need for that day on your desk. Other than that, your desk should be completely clear. Take a few minutes to:

- ✧ delete old or useless computer files
- ✧ reorganize your computer files
- ✧ clean your desk
- ✧ go through old files in your file cabinet

also keep your home organized and in order. From the kitchen to your bedroom, the closets and family room, set aside a time for cleaning and organizing your home. If you have a home office that you work in, treat it just as you treat your work area. Keep it clear of unnecessary items and only have that day's tasks in the open.

✦ ✦ ✦

The Source of Negativity

This may take some soul searching, but it is key to improving your attitude. Answer the question, "Why am I negative?" Even if your overall attitude is positive, there are still times when it has a dip. The sources of these dips are also important to zero in on. If you can find the source to the negativity, your chances of a successful improvement greatly increases.

✦ ✦ ✦

Is It a Person?

If the source of your bad mood or negativity lies with a particular individual, talk with him. This is very difficult for many people, but it is also the surest way to free yourself of constant mental stress and worry. Confronting a situation head on is the simplest way to fix any issue. When you do speak with the person, be sure to do so in a non-confrontational manner.

✦ ✦ ✦

Is It a Thing?

If the cause of your problem is not a person but rather a situation or issue, work on fixing it. Sound too simple? Well, it is simple and that is why it works. After speaking with people about their attitude problems I begin to see where the cause lies. They spend all of their time thinking about their problem, telling others about their problem, and worrying about their problem. They never actually focus on fixing the problem. If you know a particular issue is weighing you down, start working on it and stop worrying about it.

✦ ✦ ✦

Information

Once you have narrowed down the source of your negativity, learn about it. For example, if you are being brought down because you are afraid of being laid off at work, get the facts about the situation. If that is not possible, you have three choices: improve your current knowledge and skill level to ensure continued employment, add to your current skill set to make yourself employable at other businesses, or do nothing and continue to worry. Obviously the latter should be avoided, but the point is that education replaces worry with informed thinking. In many cases we are afraid of things that we don't understand.

✦ ✦ ✦

The Control is Yours

You can improve your attitude, make it worse, or let it be. You can look at life with an optimistic view, or a pair of skeptical eyes. The point is, the choice is yours. I cannot make you think differently. Your friends cannot make you think differently. Your boss cannot make you think differently. Your family cannot make you think differently. Only you can do that. No matter what changes you wish to make in your life, the power is always yours. It begins with, and ends with, you.

Our attitude toward life determines life's attitude towards us.

Earl Nightingale

Revisit the Fun Things in Your Past

If you have great memories from your childhood, find a symbol that represents that moment or feeling. For example, if you loved putting models together when you were young, put a model together and put it on your desk. This will give your attitude a reminder of the good things in your past, and the good things yet to come. Try incorporating these ideas:

- ❖ old books
- ❖ old hobbies
- ❖ old neighborhoods
- ❖ old friends

Avoid the Impossible Situation

I wouldn't advise you to avoid situations as a habit, but if it is a problem that can easily be avoided without causing harm or trouble, do so. For example, if a group of employees gathers together in the morning to gossip about the rest of the company, you can avoid that group to keep your attitude positive.

✦ ✦ ✦

If All Else Fails, Move On

If you can't fix, change, or avoid a frustrating situation or problem, accept it and move on. The saying holds true, "There's no use crying over spilt milk." It is a mature mind that can look at a troublesome issue, realize nothing can be done, and move on.

✦ ✦ ✦

Small Steps to Great Changes

Start with small and simple steps. Improving something as large as your attitude can be an overwhelming process, but it doesn't have to be. If you notice that a tip you have tried works well, continue to use it and try to add another. You don't have to completely revamp your life in one day. Take it slow and you'll find that things will begin to improve.

✦ ✦ ✦

Positive Surroundings

If you notice a positive group or organization, join them. It is important to be around others who will make you better; people who bring out the best in you.

✦ ✦ ✦

You Will Not Always be Happy

This is important to understand. No matter how much you plan things out, or follow the sage advice of others, you cannot guarantee problem-free days for the rest of your life. There will be down days, and there will be up days. The important thing is the overall trend. A bad day here and there is fine, as long as it doesn't take a majority position.

✦ ✦ ✦

Take a Break

When you are mentally, physically, and emotionally worn down, take a break. It could be a quick five minute breather at the office, or a weekend getaway with your significant other. We all need a break now and then. This is also good advice when you are in a bad mood. Removing yourself from the situation for a few minutes will help to dissolve your frustrated feelings.

✦ ✦ ✦

Your Cool Down

Choose a place, both at home and at work, that is quiet, calm, and relaxing. This will be where you will go to take your quick breaks. Find a place that is far from distraction and noise. Your quiet place must be just that, quiet. If you cannot find a place at work, a walk around the block can also do the trick.

✦ ✦ ✦

What Would You Like to Improve?

Make a list of the things that you want to change about your attitude. It could be changes in how you react to typical situa-

People are just about as happy as they make up their minds to be.

Abraham Lincoln

Some Things You Can't Change

Accept factors about yourself and your environment that you cannot change. Putting time and thought into these areas is a waste of your time and will only upset you. If you are short, don't dwell on not being tall. If you are young, don't focus on growing up. If you are old, don't live in the past. Take what you have and make the best of it.

tions, or how you deal with unfriendly people. As with all change, the goal must be specific, achievable, and measurable. Before you can enjoy a confident attitude, you must know what areas you would like to improve. Prioritize your list, and start working on the first item. This is something you can begin today.

✦ ✦ ✦

What Do You Like?

Write down five to ten things that you like about your attitude. It's important to remind yourself that there are a lot of things that you like about yourself and your attitude. You aren't starting from ground zero.

✦ ✦ ✦

Wasted Worry

If the situation is out of your control, let it go. A great deal of the things we worry about are in the hands of someone else. What good does it really do to stress over something like this? None at all. When you separate things you can control from those that you cannot, you will be lifting a great weight off your shoulders.

✦ ✦ ✦

The Step-Back System

Here is a technique you can use to fully appreciate special moments in your life.

1. **Realize You're in the Moment**—The first step is to realize that you are in the middle of something good. It could be a beautiful day on your family vacation, or a perfect afternoon with your children. You are the judge

of what moments you'd like to appreciate.

2. **Take a Step Back**—This is the main part of the system. Once you realize you are experiencing a moment you'd like to have last forever, stop yourself for a moment and take a Step Back. Take yourself away from the situation. Take a short walk, a quick break, or simply close your eyes. Once you are removed from the situation, think about it as if it happened in the past. Picture how happy you were, the details of the scene, and the others around you. Feel the emotions you felt, see and hear the faces and sounds. Remember how much you enjoyed the time, and how much you'd like to enjoy it again.

3. **Make Your Entry**—Once you feel the happiness of the moment, think about this; it's no longer in the past, it's right now! You just thought about how great you felt in that past moment, and now you can live it in the present.

   You just appreciated the current moment by looking back on the situation. Once you are in the middle of the moment again, remember . . .

4. **Enjoy Yourself**—This will be a moment that, like all others, will eventually pass. With this in mind, really let it sink in. Take a look around, and realize you are in the middle of something great.

An optimist is a person who sees a green light everywhere. The pessimist sees only the red light. But the truly wise person is color blind.

Dr. Albert Schweitzer

Be a Motivational Mentor

Offer your help to a friend who is working towards a goal. Set up a general outline of the process you would like to follow. Your responsibilities may include:

- ❖ offering advice from your own experiences
- ❖ checking up daily or weekly on progress
- ❖ thinking of new ways to tackle their challenge
- ❖ setting up meetings to readjust plan of action
- ❖ motivating them
- ❖ keeping them reminded of their initial commitment
- ❖ celebrating successes

Taking a Step Back every now and then will help you appreciate life. No longer will you be someone who takes life for granted.

❖ ❖ ❖

Do Something You Love

A quick and easy way to give your attitude a boost is to take part in an activity that you love doing. It could be sports, reading, building, writing, thinking, etc. When you know you need a quick fix, set aside time in the immediate future to enjoy yourself.

❖ ❖ ❖

Maximize the Good Time

When you are feeling great get as much done as possible. When your attitude is positive you will work smarter, more effectively and more creatively. Because you don't know what tomorrow holds, it's a great way to make the most of a good thing.

❖ ❖ ❖

Smile

That's all it takes to improve your mood. Many people have said that positive movements lead to positive attitudes. For example, if you walk briskly with your head held high, you'll feel a little more confident and sure of yourself. This theory may or may not be true, but with something as simple as smiling, why not try it out?

❖ ❖ ❖

What Would a Positive Person Do?

When you need to make a decision, or respond to a problem, ask yourself what a positive person would do. Perhaps you know someone who has an attitude that you would like to emulate. Think about how they would respond and give it a try.

✦ ✦ ✦

Appreciate the Small Things

It's the small things in life that mean the most. Conversations with good friends, a great movie, or a call from your mom or dad are examples of the small things that happen in your life that really add to its value and satisfaction. Don't take the small things for granted. When you begin to look for small things to appreciate you'll spend the bulk of your time enjoying yourself with very little time left for much else.

✦ ✦ ✦

Family Pictures

Put a family picture on your desk. When you are working with your nose to the grindstone it's easy to become lost in the heap of work. Putting a picture of your family on your desk in the office or home will serve as a quick reminder about what is really important.

✦ ✦ ✦

The Positive People

When you need to feel better, call up a friend who is known for being positive and supportive. We all know someone who has the gift of making a terrible situation seem manageable. Aside from lifting your spirits, you will also be able to learn from their method of making things better.

✦ ✦ ✦

The greatest discovery of my generation is that human beings can alter their lives by altering their attitudes of mind.

William James

Sounding Board

It's important to have a good friend who is willing to listen to you and your ideas. It is also important to remember to offer to listen to their ideas as well. When you find someone who is willing to offer support and advice, don't let go. They will come in handy more times than you think.

Don't Hold a Grudge

It's not healthy, it's not worth it, and it serves no purpose in your life. You have two choices with a grudge; you can either confront the situation head on and try to fix it, or forget about it completely.

✦ ✦ ✦

Spend Time with Children

If you have children of your own, this is a simple task. If not, visit a friend or family member who has children. The power of kids is amazing. Spending only a few minutes around or with them can improve your mood in seconds. They have a very simple way of looking at things, which can help to simplify your views about the problems, challenges, and obstacles you face in your life.

✦ ✦ ✦

Hold a Baby

This may sound like an odd tip to improve your attitude, but I have personally seen people do a complete turnaround when they hold a baby in their arms. Everything that you were worrying about, stressing about or getting upset over fades away as your focus narrows in on only one thing, that precious little life.

✦ ✦ ✦

Picnic in the Park

If you can leave for lunch at work, try having a small picnic in the park. This is a great way to relax outdoors, enjoy the weather, and give your mind and body a well-deserved break. You can also try this on the weekends with your family. Set aside a picnic date and let everyone in the family know about it. When the time comes, get your supplies together, make the trip, and enjoy a wonderful day in the sun with your loved ones.

✦ ✦ ✦

Teach

Step into the role of teacher and help another individual learn something new. The process of teaching is very fulfilling, fun, and exciting. You also get to see the opposite viewpoint of a situation. You can help your spouse learn something new, teach your children, or even help your friends when they need to learn about something you know a lot about.

✦ ✦ ✦

Anticipation

Anticipating a future event is sometimes better than the event itself. When you have something to look forward to, you have a very powerful attitude tool. For instance, you just got the loan you needed for your first home. Moving is something very exciting to look forward to. A few days later, you receive a bill in the mail for something you didn't even order. Quite frustrating, but you have a secret weapon. Instead of getting upset over the error in billing you focus on your new home. The bill doesn't seem so bad now. When you keep your focus on the upcoming event that you are excited about, some problems don't matter as much. As long as you have something good to look forward to, you won't mind the small problems that come your way.

✦ ✦ ✦

When we are flat on our backs there is no way to look but up.

Roger Babson

Benefits of Action

There are many benefits to becoming fit and increasing the amount of movement you do during the day. Among them are:

- ✧ better sleep
- ✧ improvement in stamina
- ✧ improvement in your cardiovascular system
- ✧ body movement with greater ease and less tension

Look at Old Photographs

A photo album can take you back to some wonderful times. It's a simple way to go back into the past and relive your most precious moments. Set aside some time this week to go through old pictures by yourself or with the rest of the family. You could even bring them to work and share your stories with others.

✦ ✦ ✦

A Relaxing Hobby

We have talked about the importance of having a hobby, but it is equally important to have a soothing pastime to use as a relaxing activity. If your hobby is basketball you may have a hard time relaxing during a game. Several relaxing activities include reading, walking, drawing, playing music, or writing.

✦ ✦ ✦

Volunteer

There is no better way to give back to your fellow human beings than to volunteer your time and energy. The options for volunteering are endless and the one that you choose must be compatible with your lifestyle and values. Regardless of what road you take, be sure to offer your hand to others. Only when we give, do we truly receive.

✦ ✦ ✦

Baby-sit

To enjoy the fun things about kids try baby-sitting. It's an easy and profitable way to have fun and act like a kid again. Better yet, do it for free!

✦ ✦ ✦

Give Blood

Every year, thousands of people require blood to survive and live healthy lives. It only takes a few hours of your time and a blood donation to save a life. Contact your local blood drive and set up a time to donate. You'll be able to give back and help someone continue living a normal life.

✦ ✦ ✦

Donate Clothing

When you have extra clothes around the house that have no use, donate them. Go through your clothes, your significant other's clothes, as well as your children's things. If you no longer have use for certain items, offer them to those in need.

✦ ✦ ✦

Organize a Food Drive

Another great way to give back to others is putting together a food drive. Find a group of businesses, organizations, or clubs that would like to take part in a food drive. You could also run one exclusively through your company. You may not be able to bring in the amounts of food that large, nationally supported drives can, but it doesn't matter. Any amount you can raise is extremely helpful to those who need it most.

✦ ✦ ✦

Donate Money to Charities

If you have the means to do so, donate to charities that you believe in. Without financial or volunteer support, many of the charities that help thousands of people throughout

Always look at what you have left. Never look at what you have lost.

Robert H. Schuller

Integrity

Do what is right simply because you know it is right.

the world would cease to exist. The next time the thought of donating comes to you, don't let the notion simply slip away. Get information, make contact, and help.

✦ ✦ ✦

Join a Local Club or Organization

An even better way to help your community is to become a member of a charitable organization in which you are interested. Food drives, paper drives, food shelters, and many more organizations need people to make them work. Locate the group that you believe strongly in and take the necessary steps to join their ranks.

✦ ✦ ✦

Have One Joke to Share

People love to laugh. During the week keep your eyes open for a good joke to share with your friends and family. Not only will you make someone's day better, but you'll also share in their laughter.

✦ ✦ ✦

The Feel Good Story

When you come across a really great story that you want to remember, write it down. The next day at work or at home, share the story with others. If done well, this will have the same effect as a good joke. It will lift the spirits of both the speaker and listener, and maybe even pass on an important lesson.

✦ ✦ ✦

Become a Big Brother or Big Sister

What better way to help out another person than to give them your time, thought, and energy on a consistent basis. The impact that this organization has on the lives of thousands of young girls and boys is amazing. You can truly change a life when you become a part of this process.

✦ ✦ ✦

De-clutter

Clean up messes around the house. When you have a cluttered environment it's hard to feel at ease and positive. Take five minutes to go through the house and put things in their place. Once your home is clear, your mind will be as well.

✦ ✦ ✦

Give Your House a Makeover

Dedicate one day during the weekend to give your house the white glove treatment. Leave no stone unturned, no mess untidy. Cleaning your home is a way of cleaning out your mind. Being surrounded by clutter can drag your attitude down. It's hard to get enthusiastic when everything around you is screaming confusion. Once your home is exactly how you like it, you'll have an easier time doing the same with your attitude.

✦ ✦ ✦

Attitude & The Internet

Sit down in your computer chair, connect to the Internet, and type 'Attitude' into a search engine. In return you'll get a million pages that may or may not match your exact needs. Chances are good that you'll be able to find quite a few helpful resources among these sites. You may find useful tips, insightful articles, or viewpoints you hadn't otherwise considered.

There is little difference in people, but that little difference makes a big difference. The little difference is attitude. The big difference is whether it is positive or negative.

W. Clement Stone

Honesty

Though it may not be easy, be honest with yourself and others.

Your Furniture

Rearrange the furniture in your house. This is a simple way to refresh your environment and your attitude. Better yet, get your family members to do the moving for you and sit back and enjoy the show.

✦ ✦ ✦

Movement is Key

If you feel drained of energy and are in no mood to be happy, get moving. Movement is key to changing your mood. Take a walk, shuffle papers, or grab a quick snack. When you begin to move and get your blood flowing, you will again become alert and motivated to get going.

✦ ✦ ✦

Put a Radio in the Bathroom

For an energized morning, bring a radio into the bathroom with you while you take your shower. Instead of dragging your body into the shower, you'll have music, audio programs, or morning radio shows perking you up and helping you to come alive. Put the radio in a safe place! You may like it near you, but putting a radio next to the tub is a bad idea. You can also find shower safe radios that hang right on the nozzle.

✦ ✦ ✦

Respond vs. React

In the world of attitude, this is a big one. The difference between responding and reacting to a situation is the difference between being negative and positive. When anything happens that directly or indirectly affects you, a choice is made. You either respond to the situation, or you react to it. Reacting includes reflex-like emotion that comes without prior thought. It is the first thing that comes naturally. Responding is logical. It is thinking twice before you act once. The process of responding includes taking in the facts of the situation, looking at your options, choosing the best option, and putting it into action. For example, if you can't get a key to work in your lock you can scream, yell, and throw a fit, or find out why it's not working. After inspection you may even find that you were using the wrong key. Respond to life, don't react. This alone can improve your attitude tenfold.

It's your attitude, not your aptitude, that determines your altitude in life.

Michael Aun

✦ ✦ ✦

Tape Up Birthday Cards

When you receive cards from friends and family, don't just throw them away or put them in a drawer. Choose a wall in your home and tape them up. You can also place them all on a counter, mantle, or desk. This is a simple reminder that you have people out there who care about you.

✦ ✦ ✦

Go to See a Comedian

If laughter is the best medicine, then why not go to a laugh doctor? Check the local paper for comedians or check out the comedy club in town. This is a guaranteed way to make you laugh, feel better, and have fun.

✦ ✦ ✦

The Grass is Always Greener . . .

You may wish things were different in your life, but there are others who have what you

Courage

Have the courage to break free from comfort and reach for challenging heights.

want, and want what you have. The trouble with people is that they take what they have for granted, and usually want something else. When they get what they think they desired, they want what they already had. Sound a little confusing? I think so too. Make it easier on yourself and appreciate the things that you currently have in your life.

✦ ✦ ✦

Break the Routine

If, after using these tips and more, you can't seem to find a solution to your attitude predicament, break the routine. If mornings are especially difficult for you, do something totally out of the ordinary the next day. If you can't seem to get motivated to work on a project at work, change your work routine and look at it from a totally different view.

✦ ✦ ✦

Daydream

When possible, have fun daydreaming. Let your thoughts wander and think of the great things you will accomplish in your future. Get excited about the goals you'll reach, the dreams you'll achieve, and the life you're going to live. Try not to make a habit of this while on the job or taking part in physical activities, it could get dangerous.

✦ ✦ ✦

The Letter Never Sent

From Abe Lincoln to Mark Twain, men and women have used this technique to get things off their chests, vent, and lift the weight from their shoulders. If something is bothering you or something is exciting you, write a letter to a friend about it. Hold nothing back. After you are finished, simply file the letter away or throw it in the trash. The process is the key here, not the final product.

✦ ✦ ✦

Leave Behind a Clean House

Before you leave for work in the morning be sure to make the beds, straighten up the bathroom and kitchen, and leave your house knowing everything is in order. It will help you to leave with a crisp attitude and at night you will return to an organized house. Leaving it a mess and returning to that mess is no way to start or end your day.

✦ ✦ ✦

No-Negativity Day

Choose one day each week to be free of negativity. When something happens to you that would normally set off a bit of anger, let it go and move on. In time, try to extend your no-negativity day to two or three days. You'll begin to see that on your no-negativity days you get along better with others, are in a better mood, and feel mentally and physically stronger.

✦ ✦ ✦

"Call Me On It"

Inform your friends that you want to be told when you are acting negatively. Most times, your friends will keep their distance and stay quiet when you are in a 'mood'. If you let them know that you are trying to improve your attitude and they should let you know if you slip up, they will most likely be more than willing to help. The tricky part is taking their

If you don't like something change it. If you can't change it, change your attitude. Don't complain.

Maya Angelou

Hope

The future is what you make of it and it will be brighter if you look on it with a hopeful eye.

constructive criticism at the time of the negative remark, attitude, or reaction. Be open-minded and willing to listen to their advice.

✦ ✦ ✦

Sing in the Shower

What a way to start the day! For you, it will get the energy flowing, get you pumped up, and start the day off great. For those listening to you, it may do just the opposite. Too bad. The morning is your time to shine. Choose a song that you love, jump in the shower, and let it rip.

✦ ✦ ✦

Garden

Gardening is both therapeutic and rewarding. If you are new to the world of gardening, ask around for help or look on the Internet for quick information. You can also start small and get the desired effect. You don't need to grow the Hanging Gardens to enjoy growing flowers and foods.

✦ ✦ ✦

Once a Day, Thank Away

Each day think of one thing that you are thankful for. Your kids, husband or wife, your health, your attitude, your career, etc. Remembering what you are thankful for will keep you grateful for today, and hopeful about tomorrow.

✦ ✦ ✦

Memorize Favorite Quotes

When you come across a quotation that captures the thoughts and feelings you have perfectly, memorize that quotation and pass it along to others. Quotations are powerful. They can lift the spirit, and inspire others to greatness. Keep the great ones fresh in your mind.

✦ ✦ ✦

The Selfless Act

The philosophical debate over the selfless act will continue for as long as people walk the Earth. Some say it is impossible to do something that is completely unselfish, while others say it is not. For our purposes here, it's possible. Try to commit one selfless act each week or month. The prerequisites are simply to do something kind for which you expect nothing in return.

✦ ✦ ✦

Be Polite

Hold doors for strangers, help others when you see they need it, and say thank you. This is just another area of a positive outlook on life. The values and morals you carry with you are best demonstrated by your actions towards others. If you feel good on the inside, let it show on the outside.

✦ ✦ ✦

Flip a Coin

Indecision is a stress causing problem, but it doesn't have to be. For decisions that are of little importance, flip a coin and go with the decision. This simple tip will cut down on unnecessary time spent on trivial matters. Flip a coin to keep your simple decisions simple.

✦ ✦ ✦

The Decision Matrix

When the decision you have to make holds more weight than a coin flip can solve, all

> *Win as if you were used to it, lose as if you enjoyed it for a change.*
>
> *Eric Golnik*

Perseverance

The first try will most likely result in failure. This cannot be enough to keep you down. Never give up and stick with your goals until the end.

you need is a sheet of paper and a pencil. Draw a line down the center of the sheet, labeling one side 'advantages' and the other 'disadvantages'. Write the decision you have to make at the top. Then, list the advantages and disadvantages of each option. When finished, you should have a clearer picture of what each path will produce. The decision making process won't be as difficult if you put a little effort into this quick and easy system.

✦ ✦ ✦

Positive Talk

Certain words need to be erased from your vocabulary if you want to make the improvement process as easy as possible. Replace words such as frustrated, angry, negative, mad, unfair, unlucky, and failure with positive words like challenge, opportunity, positive, solution, and understanding. The words you use on a daily basis have a major impact on your attitude. You may not even be aware of how you impact others, but your words will speak volumes to those around you. Be aware of your vocabulary, what tone you want to set, and how you are currently communicating. If there isn't a match between what you want and what you are doing, start to replace negative phrases with positive ones.

✦ ✦ ✦

Hang Up a Punching Bag

This tip may involve a little more than changing your vocabulary or writing down a wishlist, but it's a useful tip just the same. Expelling tension from the body with physical activity is a great way to change your attitude. Create a small workout room in your basement, purchase a set of weights, or hang up a punching bag. You'll be in great physical and mental shape.

✦ ✦ ✦

Failure is Not a Person

Remember when you or anyone you know fails, it is an event and not the person. You can fail a thousand times, but that does not make you a failure. Only when you admit defeat and give up trying does failure become a trait. Never give up, no matter what, and you will succeed. I guarantee that. You'll find a way to make it work, and you'll be happy you kept with it until success was reached. Failure is an event, not a person.

✦ ✦ ✦

Become a Mr. or Ms. Fix-It

When something small goes wrong in the house, being able to fix it on your own is a great feeling. When you know the basics of home repair, you get a sense of confidence and capability. Strength and confidence are pillars of a positive attitude, and this simple process can add to both of these founding principles. You can get information about home repair from bookstores, the Internet, library, or friends. The resources are limitless, all you need to do is look for them.

✦ ✦ ✦

The Problem Becomes a Challenge

Problems are bad, troublesome, frustrating, negative things that we try to avoid. Challenges are fun, exciting, and motivating opportunities that we look forward to. The funny part? They are the same thing. It all

> *What counts is not necessarily the size of the dog in the fight, it's the size of the fight in the dog.*
>
> Dwight D. Eisenhower

Belief

You can, and will, do whatever you wish to do.

depends on how you look at it. When something happens that you don't especially prefer, think of it as a challenge and look for solutions.

✦ ✦ ✦

Care Packages for the Needy

This is an activity that you and your family can share together. To begin, find a small box or bucket strong enough to hold several items. Then gather together food, clothes, or other things that you would like to give. After putting together your care package, bring it to a local shelter to offer to someone in need.

✦ ✦ ✦

Create a Success File for the Home

Create a file to place your successes and cherished items. You can include pictures drawn by your kids, notes from your friends and family, or certificates or awards that recognize personal achievement. When you are feeling down you can refer to your success file for a quick boost.

✦ ✦ ✦

Expectations

If you find yourself feeling defeated or disappointed over your shortcomings it may be time to take a look at the expectations you set for yourself. Write out the things at which you are failing. When finished, show your list to your spouse or a close friend. After talking things out you will most likely realize that you have set your expectations too high. Also, once on paper the things you are having trouble with won't seem as bad.

✦ ✦ ✦

You Cannot Control Others

A source of attitude problems stems from individuals trying to change other people. Let's face it, people are resistant to change. This means that in order for you to create a life that you enjoy and find positive, you have to focus on changing yourself. If you don't like a situation, think of how you can change to improve it. Let go of the notion that you can control the thoughts and actions of others and you'll find your attitude improving and your stress decreasing immediately.

Attitudes are contagious. Is yours worth catching?

Author Unknown

19

Energy Boost

A LL OF THE TIPS, techniques, and ideas you are reading won't be of any use to you if you don't have the energy to put them into play. A lack of energy and alertness can take its toll on your motivation, stress levels, and attitude. The good news is you can increase your energy. With the right changes in your lifestyle, you can wake up with energy and keep it going throughout the rest of the day.

No longer will you have to feel tired or sluggish during your waking hours. Increasing and maintaining a high energy level isn't hard to do, and you can make improvements starting today. The tips and ideas that follow will help you discover what your current energy levels are and how to improve upon them.

Start with Activity

Start the day with a physical activity. This will get your blood flowing, your brain working, and your body moving. The activities don't have to be intense, just enough to move your muscles and your mind. Examples include:

- ❖ check the mail
- ❖ get the newspaper
- ❖ make breakfast
- ❖ clean the house
- ❖ get everyone else awake
- ❖ morning exercise

Mental Inventory

Take a second every now and then to take a mental inventory. Is your brain tired? Mental stress and exhaustion can weigh heavily upon your moods and overall attitude. Be aware of your current state. That will make improving your attitude much easier.

❖ ❖ ❖

Physical Inventory

The counterpart to your mental state is your physical state. Your energy and mood will obviously take a dip when you are physically tired. If you find that your energy is lacking and you are especially irritable, think about how your body feels. You may just need a quick break or change of pace.

❖ ❖ ❖

Food for Thought

Maintain a healthy diet. If you want energy, you need fuel. A healthy and well-balanced diet is necessary for energy and a positive attitude. You simply can't function correctly without one. If you frequently skip meals or eat unhealthy foods, and you desire more energy, make changes in your diet.

❖ ❖ ❖

Sleep

Get six to eight hours of good sleep per night. When you stay up late and get up early you will not be able to function properly. Your body is like any other machine; it requires rest after a long day of work and activity.

❖ ❖ ❖

Oversleeping

Make sure you don't get too much sleep. This can cause the same problems as not getting enough sleep. If you feel that you are sleeping too much, try getting up one hour earlier three days a week. After your body adjusts increase the number of early days.

✦ ✦ ✦

Exercise to Improve Your Energy

A healthy body is more than necessary for energy, it's critical. Without exercise the body becomes easily tired and exhausted. Contact a professional to help you create a simple and consistent exercise program to maximize your energy.

✦ ✦ ✦

The Nightly Check-In

Take account of how you feel just before you go to bed. If you find it difficult to sleep at night due to excessive energy or alertness, you may need to make some adjustments in your daily schedule. The same holds if you are extremely exhausted at night.

✦ ✦ ✦

Stretch

Take five to ten minutes to stretch in the morning, afternoon, or night. Muscle tension causes headaches, aches and pains in the body, and lack of concentration. Doing simple stretches during the day will help to alleviate these symptoms and give you added energy.

✦ ✦ ✦

Life expectancy would grow by leaps and bounds if green vegetables smelled as good as bacon.

Doug Larson

Candy

Sweets may give you short-term energy, but after a while their effects wear off and you're left with less energy than when you started. Keep the candy and junk food to a minimum.

Morning Check-In

How is your energy in the morning? Are you alert, awake, and ready for the upcoming day? If not, you need to make changes. Examine your diet, exercise and sleeping patterns. You will most likely find the cause of your lack of energy lies in one of these three areas.

✦ ✦ ✦

Healthy Snacks

Keep a healthy snack with you for quick energy boosts. An apple, orange, or bagel are just some of the simple but effective snacks you could carry with you in your purse or briefcase.

✦ ✦ ✦

Relax

A quick fifteen minute nap during your day will give your mind and body time to refresh and gives you a second wind for the rest of your day. Make use of the fifteen minute power nap in the home, office, or wherever you may need one.

✦ ✦ ✦

The Early Bird

If you like to get up early with a lot of energy, start with exercise and a healthy breakfast. The exercise will give you the energy you desire and the healthy breakfast will help you to sustain it throughout the rest of the day.

✦ ✦ ✦

Midday Motivation

If you find that most of your work is accomplished in the afternoon, take time to stretch for five to ten minutes in the middle of your workday. This will help to relieve muscle tension and refresh your mind.

✦ ✦ ✦

The Night Owl

If you find that most of your productive time falls at night, try to avoid exercise and stress such as paying bills. This type of activity will keep you up all night long. Instead, read a book or listen to a calming CD. This will give you the desired amount of energy. It will also make falling asleep much easier.

✦ ✦ ✦

Energy Foods

Try eating pasta, pretzels, or bagels for a quick snack. Both have the nutrients necessary for extended energy. Keep the toppings and unhealthy extras such as butter or cream cheese to a minimum.

✦ ✦ ✦

Vitamin B

Looking for more energy during the day? Try including mushrooms in your diet. They are high in vitamin B which releases the energizing hormone adrenaline into the body.

Your big opportunity may be right where you are now.

Napoleon Hill

20

Have Fun!

L AUGHTER IS, AND ALWAYS WILL BE, the best medicine around. That is why you must find ways to enjoy yourself and have fun. It not only improves your health but also has a positive impact on your attitude.

It can seem like there is no place for fun in your schedule. With all of the deadlines and demands on your time, having fun doesn't always fit into the schedule. That's why this next section has quick and easy ways to have fun, along with some more elaborate ideas.

Did You Know?

Laughter really is good medicine. Studies have shown that laughing:

✧ boosts your immune system response

✧ increases breathing capacity

✧ increases your heart rate

✧ acts as an aerobic activity

✧ causes the pituitary gland to decrease the release of stress causing chemicals

✧ reduces strain on the upper neck muscles

Celebrate

Throw a party! You don't have to have a good reason why, but if you do, all the better. Invite your friends over for dinner, or ask your co-workers over for a work party. It's all about having fun. Establish quarterly parties at work, or throw a party every time your children reach a major goal. The more opportunities you can find to have a celebration, the better.

✦ ✦ ✦

Get a Health Club Membership

This one tackles a lot of our lessons. A great deal of your health goals can be accomplished at a health club, along with having a good time with your friends. With basketball and racquetball courts in many clubs, along with indoor tracks and swimming pools, it's hard not to enjoy yourself. Check into a membership for you and your whole family today.

✦ ✦ ✦

Story Time

Great story tellers can entertain, inspire, and amaze their listeners. Develop your storytelling skills and give your family and friends a treat. If you have no original stories as of yet, the library is packed with books that contain excellent stories for you to use. It's just another way to enjoy yourself while you spend time with others.

✦ ✦ ✦

It's Time to Grow Down

You have been told to grow up for the majority of your life, and now it's time to act young.

When your children, or your friend's children, are playing don't simply watch them, get in there and play. If there ever were experts in the area of playing and having fun, it's kids. Get down on your hands and knees, remember what it's like to be a kid, and have a blast.

✦ ✦ ✦

Family Fun Night

The perfect time to put the above tips into play is the Family Fun Night. Once a week or once a month organize a night when your entire family comes together for a few hours to take part in fun activities. This will give everyone time to enjoy themselves and will build a stronger family unit.

✦ ✦ ✦

Play Board Games

The board game market is exploding. There are so many options out there that promise to offer a great time to all that play. From the older, traditional games, to the newer fast-paced ones, you'll have a lot of fun playing board games with your family and neighbors.

✦ ✦ ✦

Weekly Routine

Get three to four other families together for a board game night once a week. Ask your neighbors and close friends to join in. Rotate whose home you hold these at, and maybe even add a dinner element in the mix. You'll have fun, food, and enjoy the company of your friends and neighbors.

✦ ✦ ✦

We're fools whether we dance or not, so we might as well dance.

Japanese Proverb

Play an Instrument

If you can play an instrument, do so when you need to have a little fun. Even better, put on a little concert for your friends and family. Aside from playing at parties or gatherings, you could also sing your kids to sleep with personal songs that you have written just for them.

✦ ✦ ✦

Try Something New

Trying something new is both educating and exciting. It keeps the mind thinking, your curiosity peaking, and is a lot of fun. Make it a point in your life to try something new each month. This includes trying new foods, playing a musical instrument, or learning a new hobby. What you choose isn't the important part, it's simply choosing something to do that is the key. Have fun, and learn something new!

✦ ✦ ✦

Crazy Hair Day

If you have enough hair to be crazy with, then create a crazy hair day in your home or office. If you have daughters, I'm sure they'll have many different ideas to work with. After the hairstyle creation has concluded, get out the camera and save the day for eternity. Make sure to hide the negatives and pictures from those you respect.

✦ ✦ ✦

Clash Day in the Home

If you have kids, they may already think that your fashion sense is appalling. Now it's time to really lay it on. Organize a family clash day and make an event out of the occasion. On a Saturday or Sunday, get together the craziest clothes you own and pile them on the living room floor. One by one, let your family members choose an article of clothing. When the pile has been depleted, get into your new outfit and get on that catwalk. Again, a camera is ideal for these family fun activities.

Laughter is a tranquilizer with no side effects.

Arnold Glasow

❖ ❖ ❖

Watch a Comedy with the Family

Rent one of your favorite funny movies from the video store, buy some popcorn, and you've got a perfectly planned movie night. You'll get the opportunity to spend time with your kids and significant other, have fun watching one of your favorite movies, and take a break from the normal stress and hectic pace of the working world. To make it more democratic, you can have a different family member choose the video or DVD each week.

❖ ❖ ❖

Whistle

It's easy, most everyone can do it, and it's a direct result of choosing to be in a good mood.

❖ ❖ ❖

Learn those Words

Instead of mumbling your way through the songs you hear on the radio, learn the words to the ones you like most. Singing along with songs may annoy others, but for you, it's fun. Sing away and enjoy yourself.

❖ ❖ ❖

A Joke a Day

Sign up for an e-mail joke service. You can have a new joke emailed to you every day.

Try a New Recipe

It's simple, quick, and not only spices up dinner but also your life. Get some ideas from a friend, a television cooking show, or a cookbook. Offering the same old thing for dinner can lead to a 'same old thing' attitude. Try something new and have fun with it.

✦ ✦ ✦

Family Band Night

This one takes a little more courage, but it can be a lot of fun for the whole family. You'll need a stereo, favorite CD, tennis racquets or some other guitar shaped object, wooden or plastic spoons for drums, and a pepper shaker for the microphone. You may also want to get out the camcorder. Put on the CD, give each family member an instrument, and you have yourself a complete air-band.

✦ ✦ ✦

Act Out Books

If your children are fond of a particular kid's story, give each of them parts and act the story out. You can have fun thinking of costumes, accents, and scenery. This is a simple and fun way to spend time with your kids and enjoy each other's creativity and company.

✦ ✦ ✦

Play Sports

Set aside time for sports and active games. One of the best ways to relax and enjoy yourself is to call up your friends, head to the gym, and play. You get exercise, fun, friends, and an improved attitude.

✦ ✦ ✦

It's Only a Game

For the overly competitive athlete, sports can create unhealthy negativity. Remember that winning is a fine goal, but not at the cost of anger or frustration. You play sports to have fun and that should be the outcome as well. Challenge yourself to do better but do not criticize yourself or others for poor performance.

✦ ✦ ✦

Movies

Go to a movie. It's a simple way to enjoy yourself and get lost in a good story for two hours.

✦ ✦ ✦

Photo Time

While shopping with your children or significant other, take time to jump in a photo booth for some pictures. For a very inexpensive price you'll have fun and a photo to remember the time for years to come.

✦ ✦ ✦

Broaden Your View

Part of having fun is thinking of new and different things to do, see, and experience. That is why a great tip to having more fun in your life is to broaden your view of what fun is. A limiting idea of fun can make it difficult for you to really enjoy yourself. You don't only have to play games or go to a movie to have fun. Be creative.

People rarely succeed unless they have fun in what they are doing.

Dale Carnegie

21

Stress & Time Management

IT SEEMS THAT THERE IS ALWAYS too much stress and never enough time. These two pressures will soon wear your attitude and motivation down until there is little left. Stress can play an important role in your health and longevity. Taking steps to reduce your stress levels will improve your energy and attitude. It will also allow you to feel calm in the midst of chaos.

It is also very important to manage your time wisely. Aside from decreasing your stress and tension, using your time effectively will help you to accomplish more in less time. Together, the skills of stress and time management will equip you with the tools necessary for a successful and happy life.

Sunday Cooking System

On Sunday, cook all the next week's meals. Place them in containers and refrigerate. When their day comes, reheat and serve. This will save you on cooking time, decision time, and cleaning time.

Your Workload

Decrease your workload. Work is not the only cause of stress, but it does make up a great deal of it. If you find that you are stressed out, look first to your work schedule. Decreasing the amount of work is something that many of us would jump at, but that usually isn't so easy to carry out. Plan your work over longer periods of time, delegate your responsibilities to others, or simply abandon tasks that are unnecessary.

✦ ✦ ✦

Deep Breathing

When you feel the tension building up, take ten deep breaths. Focus on both the inhale and exhale. With each breath out, relax. Let go for a few moments and just think about your breathing. This will dissolve your immediate frustration, giving you the opportunity to look at the situation with clarity.

✦ ✦ ✦

Arrange Files Alphabetically

The time it takes to find files can add up fast. Simply arranging them alphabetically will let you find files quickly and easily. It will also allow others to find the necessary files without asking for your assistance.

✦ ✦ ✦

Arrange Files by Category

Put all like files together. If you keep related items in one place, you will be able to retrieve the desired information in half the time it normally takes. It may take some time to redo your system, but you'll know where each file goes and where to find it in less time.

✦ ✦ ✦

Balance Your Checkbook

Take a seat in the kitchen, get out your check-book and receipts, and balance your check-book. This simple process will bring relief to your mind. It gives you a chance to bring balance to your life.

✦ ✦ ✦

Clean the House

An excellent way to de-stress is to give your home a quick cleaning. Stray items or untidy areas can make it difficult to feel calm and balanced. Take a few minutes to go through the rooms in your house and tidy them up.

✦ ✦ ✦

The Pending Decision

Is an upcoming decision adding worry to your life? If so, make the decision now. A pending decision can easily add stress to your life up until the final day. Shorten the distance to the decision and make it now. You'll be free of the stress and worry, and can then get to work on what has been decided.

✦ ✦ ✦

Change Your Deadlines

Some deadlines are final, and some are not. If you have certain deadlines that you can change, perhaps giving yourself a little extra time is just what you need to calm your nerves. For example, if you have set a personal deadline of one month to reach a goal, give yourself two months if you think that

The art of being wise is the art of knowing what to overlook.

William James

The Time Cushion

Allow for a little more time with activities that don't have a definite beginning and finish. This will eliminate the mad dashes to and from work, home, soccer practice, band practice, etc.

deadline is too short. A little rescheduling will go a long way to reduce stress in your life.

✦ ✦ ✦

The Stress Releaser

If you don't have a stress releaser, you need to get one today. What is it? It's simply a physical activity that helps you release built up stress. You could play basketball, run, or work out. The important thing is to choose an activity that is physical. Reading or cooking won't do the trick. So when the stress is building, fight back with your very own stress releaser!

✦ ✦ ✦

Stress at Work

When the majority of stress results from work-related activities, set up a meeting with your boss. In many cases, he has most likely been through the same situations. Your boss may know exactly how it feels to have unending responsibilities and duties to take care of. Because of this, he may know of some great tips to help reduce your stress level.

✦ ✦ ✦

Work with Better Tools

A small, but important, area of stress comes from the tools you have to work with. For example, using old or out of date machinery can add stress and frustration to the job. Working with a malfunctioning computer can also make work very difficult to enjoy. If it's the tools you work with that cause stress, look into updating them.

✦ ✦ ✦

Involve Others in the Project

If the project or task is too much for one person to handle, get others involved in the process. If the chores at home are overwhelming, include your kids or significant other. If your position at work demands the effort of two or three people, look into adding a worker.

✦ ✦ ✦

The Consistently Stressful Situation

Many people have a stressful situation that comes into their lives on a consistent basis. Most often, the focus is not on solving the problem but on the symptoms of that problem. Perhaps you become stressed when a customer complaint is handed to you, or when your kids don't clean up their messes. Put your time and energy into looking at the situation logically and coming up with a solution. Eliminate the cause and you eliminate the stress.

✦ ✦ ✦

The Pre-Stress Syndrome

An upcoming talk with an employee, a meeting with the boss, or a visit from the new in-laws; these and many more potentially stressful situations cause trouble for people long before they actually occur. Don't let this happen to you! Take care of the situation when the time comes, not days or weeks before. The worrying you do beforehand will not improve the situation at all. Save your mind and body from unnecessary stress and worry of future events.

✦ ✦ ✦

Health is the greatest of all possessions; a pale cobbler is better than a sick king.

Isaac Bickerstaff

Junk the Mail

As soon as you get junk mail or decide you don't need a particular document, throw it away.

When It's Over, It's Over

The time has come and gone, but you still find yourself fretting over a troublesome situation. The words that you wish you said keep running in your mind, minute after minute, hour after hour. This is a common and extremely stressful habit. You must be able to let go of what has already happened, and move on. If there is nothing left for you to do, accept it and look ahead.

✦ ✦ ✦

Who's Causing Your Stress?

If a person is causing your stress, talk with them about it. This is easier said than done, but no one said doing the right thing was always going to be easy. Confronting the person who is causing you stress may be uncomfortable in the short-term, but it will create a long-term solution. Be careful to not be excessively critical when you communicate. Begin and end the conversation on a positive note.

✦ ✦ ✦

Reality Check

This isn't easy to admit, but the stress you deal with could be due in part to your own actions. If you are negative to your co-workers, they may return the same attitude. Can you think of situations where this may be happening? Take an honest look at your attitude and your actions. You may find the real cause to your stress and tension.

✦ ✦ ✦

The Brain Drain

Take time each day to let your mind relax. Keep negative thoughts and stressful worries out of the picture. You can either focus on positive, uplifting thoughts or none at all. Much like your body, your mind needs a break now and then.

✦ ✦ ✦

Positive Pays

As we have seen in many other situations, a positive attitude is key. If trouble arises you can accept it and begin to think of solutions, or you can worry about the implications of the problem. The latter will cause you stress and worry, while the former will bring excitement and enthusiasm. The choice is yours.

✦ ✦ ✦

Get It Out

With all the thoughts in your head it's no wonder you have some stress in your life. Just one day's amount of things to remember can have quite an impact on your attitude and stress levels. The solution is in getting the thoughts from your head into workable forms.

✦ ✦ ✦

The To-Do List

The easiest way to empty your thoughts onto paper and reduce stress is to make a to-do list. Get every thought, deadline, responsibility, demand, and task out of your head and into that list. Once there, you can eliminate, manipulate, and expand on your ideas much easier than if they were only in your head.

Prevention is better than cure.

Desiderius Erasmus

Phone Tip

Stand up when you talk on the phone. This will keep the conversations shorter and give you more time.

Give each one a plan of action, start date, and deadline. Stress-free and ready to go!

✦ ✦ ✦

Ask for Help

It's the easiest way to solve a stress problem, but often overlooked. When you feel the stress building because of your duties or obligations, ask for help. If the person you ask says no, there is no harm done. If they say yes, then you've got a real friend and less stress.

✦ ✦ ✦

Does it Really Matter?

When you are about to lose your temper or get upset, ask yourself, "Does it really matter? Will I even remember this next week?" The answer will usually be no, and you can relax and deal with the situation calmly. Take a moment to think before you act and you will find your stress dropping to an all-time low.

✦ ✦ ✦

Stretch Your Muscles

Stand up and stretch. After working all day or all afternoon your muscles need some refreshing. Take a quick walk, touch your toes, or do some jumping jacks.

✦ ✦ ✦

Stress and Pain

A recent study found that individuals with high stress levels were more sensitive to pain. Just another reason to pay attention to your stress levels and keep calm, relaxed, and in control.

✦ ✦ ✦

Squeeze and Relax

Starting at your toes, and working you way up the body, squeeze your muscles for ten seconds and then relax them. This will give your entire body relief from built up tension. Be sure to let those around you know what you are doing first. You don't want to stress others out who think you are going crazy.

✦ ✦ ✦

Music to Calm Your Nerves

Put on your headphones, sit in your favorite chair, and listen to music that helps you feel calm and peaceful. A few minutes of this soothing exercise is enough to get you back on your feet, stress-free.

✦ ✦ ✦

Swing to Relieve Stress

If you have a swing on the porch or in the backyard you have an excellent tool to relieve stress. On days when you can feel the tension building up, give yourself an hour at night to relax and swing. It has a very calming effect and can help you enjoy the rest of your evening.

✦ ✦ ✦

Your Personal Altar

Use your night stand as a place of solace and comfort. Place personal objects and symbols on it such as family photos, sentimental objects, or your favorite book. Whenever you need calm and quiet in your life, you'll have to look no further than the night stand.

✦ ✦ ✦

Trouble is only opportunity in work clothes.

Henry Kaiser

Worries

Make a list of your worries. After some time you will realize that the majority of them never materialize. That's because nearly 90% of the things we worry about never actually happen.

Sight for Sore Eyes

Looking at a soothing picture or photograph has been shown to reduce blood pressure and muscle tension within five minutes. Therefore, keep pictures you find soothing in places that cause you tension or stress. A picture in your office or home can help you start feeling more relaxed today.

✦ ✦ ✦

The Contingency Plan

Stress can come about in many ways. A common cause is a breakdown of planned events. For example, you are on your way out the door when the baby-sitter calls to say that she can't watch your daughter that night. Now what do you do? For times like these create a contingency plan just in case things fall through at the last minute. You could get a backup baby-sitter, or spend a quiet evening at home instead. The contingency plan will eliminate the mad rush to fix broken plans.

✦ ✦ ✦

Tune in to Your Breathing

When you are stressed your breathing becomes short, shallow, and erratic. Making a few simple changes in your breathing patterns can help make you feel more relaxed. Consciously slow your breathing. Through your nose, try to make your inhalations twice as long as your exhalations. Doing this for one to five minutes is enough to bring your breathing back to normal and your stress level down.

✦ ✦ ✦

Where Does the Time Go?

Until you know where your time is going, you can't begin to manage it. For one week keep track of what you do with your time. Create a simple chart listing the days of the week on one side, and one hour increments along the other. Each time you begin an activity, make a note of it on your chart. When you finish, log the total time. After one week you'll be amazed at where your time actually goes.

+ + +

The Most Productive Times

What are the most productive times of your day? Knowing this will help you to create an effective work schedule. You will want to plan complex or larger tasks during your productive times to be efficient.

+ + +

The Least Productive Times

Just as important to know as your most productive times of the day, are your least productive times. You will be able to determine if mornings or afternoons are better for you to do smaller tasks and duties.

+ + +

Urgent Tasks

Are you spending your time on urgent things that are not your responsibility? If so, you may want to cut those out of your schedule. When situations arise that demand immediate attention, you may not be the best one for the job. Doing so simply because you're there isn't a good reason. Politely decline requests to do jobs that lie outside of your responsibility.

Stress is an ignorant state. It believes that everything is an emergency.

Natalie Goldberg

Salt in the Tub

If you take baths to calm your nerves try adding a cup of salt. This will draw the lactic acid out of your system relieving muscle tension. Now a warm bath can soothe mind and body at the same time.

What Activities Need More Time?

After you have gone a week looking at your time commitments you'll notice some areas get more attention than others. Ask yourself if important areas are getting their share of your time. In many instances, the important duties do not receive adequate amounts of time and therefore cause stress and frustration in the workplace. Distribute your time wisely and focus on the important responsibilities you have.

✦ ✦ ✦

What Activities Need Less Time?

You will no doubt find that a portion of your time is spent on trivial matters. Decide which items need less time and schedule accordingly. After reviewing your time schedule you should be able to create an extremely effective and efficient timetable for the coming weeks and months.

✦ ✦ ✦

A's, B's, and C's

Make a list of all the things you spend time on during the day. Once complete, label each item with an *A*, *B*, or *C*. Your *A* items are the tasks that help you reach your goals. These activities should receive the majority of your time and attention. The *B* items help, but are not as important as your *A* list. The tasks that take away from your goals and interrupt your schedule are labeled *C*. Your job is to eliminate *C*'s, focus on *A*'s, and keep your *B*'s to a minimum.

✦ ✦ ✦

Cutting Down on C's

A second list that you can make to help with your time is the Elimination of *C*'s list. List each *C* item from your A-B-C list on a sheet of paper. Go down your list and write out ideas that could cut down on the time spent on these items. For instance, if you wrote down 'Talking with co-workers before I get working,' then perhaps setting a time limit on the amount of talking you do would be a good solution. For each *C* item, think of two to three solutions.

✦ ✦ ✦

Nature does not hurry, yet everything is accomplished.

Lao Tzu

Time is Money

How much is your time worth? When you actually affix an amount to your time and effort, you may not spend your time so haphazardly. For instance, if your time is worth $15 per hour, would you be willing to spend thirty dollars talking to a friend at the water cooler?

✦ ✦ ✦

Common Time Wasters

Common time wasters plague us all. The key is to realize that they are in our schedules and then create a plan of action to decrease or eliminate them. Several common time wasters are: lack of planning, paper shuffling, cluttered work area, afternoon tiredness, drop-in visitors, telephone, interruptions, meetings, indecision, and procrastination.

✦ ✦ ✦

Your Time Wasters

Aside from the common time wasting activities listed above, discover your own personal

The Effects of Stress

We all know that stress can cause heart trouble, muscle tension, and headaches. We all know that it is extremely unhealthy to be around stressful situations on a consistent basis, but few know of the other risks involved. Stress has been proven to increase the chances of infection, skin problems, and memory loss. It has also been shown to cause outbreaks among asthma sufferers.

time wasting habits or tendencies. If you can pinpoint your own time wasters, you will be able to create a plan of action to remedy the situation. The more you learn about yourself, the easier improvement in all areas of your life will be.

◆ ◆ ◆

Replace the Time Wasters

Once you have targeted the time wasters that have made it into your schedule, you must choose a new habit to replace them. For example, if having too many drop-in visitors is wasting your valuable time designate a set schedule of when you welcome visitors. Simply replacing your time wasting activities with new habits will more than double your efficiency.

◆ ◆ ◆

Use an Alarm

Use an alarm to keep you aware of the time and on schedule. You can use the alarm setting on your watch, a clock, or even a kitchen timer. If you would like to spend your time on a task for a specific amount of time, use a timer to keep you efficient.

◆ ◆ ◆

Your Daily Timetable

Create a timetable for each day during the week allowing for small amounts of interruptions, distractions, or other time wasting activities. Next to your planned schedule, note the actual time spent on each task. Adjust your plan at the end of the week to better match your actual needs.

◆ ◆ ◆

Wear a Watch

If you don't already have one, invest in a watch. This is the quickest and easiest way to keep track of your time. The investment for a watch is small, but the benefits are enormous.

❖ ❖ ❖

Are You Trying To Do Too Much?

Are you extending yourself beyond your abilities and time schedule? If so, you need to re-examine the available time you have along with the required demands on that time. Perhaps you need to change the amount of time you allow for certain activities. You may also need to eliminate particular activities altogether.

❖ ❖ ❖

Are You Procrastinating?

This is one of the main reasons for poor time management. Putting things off for tomorrow that you can and should complete today creates a great deal of stress and complexity for your time schedule. See the Motivation Section for tips on eliminating procrastination.

❖ ❖ ❖

Do It Right the First Time

If a decision comes to you that requires time and thought, don't rush it. Put in the time and effort it takes to make a well-informed decision. If you make rash decisions you may have to go back later and reverse the actions you've started. If you don't have time to do something twice, make sure you do it right the first time.

❖ ❖ ❖

The future is something which everyone reaches at the rate of 60 minutes an hour, whatever he does, whoever he is.

C.S. Lewis

Celery and Carrots

To calm your nerves and relax try eating some celery or carrots. Both contain the amino acid tryptophan. This chemical triggers the release of serotonin which acts to calm the brain. Just when you thought they were only for your body!

Delegate, Delegate, Delegate

Your time is scarce, valuable, and needs to be used effectively. If you spend your time away from your best skills and abilities a great waste in resources is taking place. Whenever possible, delegate tasks to others so you can spend your time where it is needed most.

✦ ✦ ✦

Meetings with a Purpose

One of the biggest time wasters in the workplace are poorly planned meetings. After people have taken their spots and finished talking about the weather, twenty minutes has already gone by. Meetings must have defined goals in order for them to be effective. Regardless of where this responsibility lies, make sure that the meetings you take part in are focused and have specific objectives.

✦ ✦ ✦

Pay Bills Online

With the introduction of online paying systems, your stress and time management skills are receiving a break. If you like doing things with less paper and no postage, look into paying your bills online. You can also have the funds taken directly from your checking or savings account. This is a quick time saver and stress reducer that you can put into place immediately.

✦ ✦ ✦

The Instant Bill System

When a bill comes in the mail, before you even take your coat off, get the checkbook out, write the check, put on the postage, and set the sealed envelope in your out box. This way you won't have bills building up.

✦ ✦ ✦

Create Routine Forms

For routine paperwork, create duplicate copies of the forms to save you time and energy. Instead of starting from scratch with each letter or correspondence, simply use one of the copies you've created.

✦ ✦ ✦

Keep Files Close

In your home office and workplace, keep files that you need often at an arm's length. This will save you more time than you think. When you have to get up to get a file or paper it can turn into quite an ordeal. Talking with co-workers, stopping by the water cooler, or being distracted by others can all be eliminated with this simple space management technique.

✦ ✦ ✦

Estimate Your Time

When you are putting together a to-do list, mark down the approximate time each task will take. This will help you to plan accordingly, put an effective list together, and keep you on track when you put it into action.

✦ ✦ ✦

Weekly Menus

To save on shopping and cooking time, plan a weekly menu for dinner. You'll head to the store knowing exactly what you need, and when you get home the whole family can help to prepare that night's choice. Taking a few

The present is a point just passed.

David Russell

Your Chair

You may not realize it, but the chair you sit in could be causing muscle tension and stress on your body. Check out where you sit or spend a great deal of your time. Lighting is also an issue. With dim lights you may be squinting to see the screen. Take steps to maintain a healthy and stress-free environment.

minutes now to plan ahead can save you hours or more in the end.

+ + +

Morning Rush

If you find yourself rushing in the morning with little to no time to get ready for work, try setting your clothes out the night before. You can also set your briefcase or bag next to the door for a quick exit.

+ + +

The Kids' Spot

Create a small area for your kids to put their hats, gloves, jackets, and book bags before they go to bed. The next morning all of their things will be in one neat place, ready to go. This will save you from searching in the morning for your son's gloves and your daughter's homework assignment.

+ + +

Extra Chairs in the Office

If you find that distractions and drop-in visitors are taking up too much of your time remove any extra chairs that are in your office. Visitors won't be as inclined to drop by and have a seat.

+ + +

Study Time

Children need to learn about time management at an early age. You can help them with this by setting aside nightly studying time. Choose a place that is quiet and free from distraction. They will learn to use their time wisely and how to study effectively.

+ + +

The Overflow

If I have a pitcher filled to the top with water I would be crazy to add an extra cup, right? The answer may be obvious but the same thing is happening in people's lives every day. They add activities to their already full schedules and can't handle the overflow. If you add something to your schedule, be sure to take something out.

✦ ✦ ✦

Just One More Thing . . .

We all know someone who always has 'just one more thing' to do before they leave. Rarely can you stick to your schedule when you keep having 'one more thing' pop up. Make it a point to be on time and leave that 'one more thing' for a later time.

✦ ✦ ✦

Trouble for Others

Lateness isn't an isolated event. When you are late for work, a party, a group function, or any other activity you are affecting each and every participant. You can and should work to reverse this habit. Many people sit back and say, "That's just the way I am." This is no excuse to pass your responsibilities to others and create problems for those you work or live with. Make an effort to drop the habit.

✦ ✦ ✦

Avoid Perfectionism

Doing things right is a good trait, to a point. When it begins to take up more time than it should you may be pushing it too far. Think

I had no shoes and complained, until I met a man who had no feet.

Indian Proverb

Caffeine

Watch your intake of caffeine. If calm is your goal, caffeine is your enemy. For a decreased stress level skip the sodas and drink water or juice.

logically when you are completing a task. Is it good as it is? Do you really need to make every aspect perfect? If not, use your time wisely and move on.

22

Attitude Interaction

RARELY IS YOUR ATTITUDE an isolated element. It is a work in progress that is constantly bombarded with outside influences. With an understanding of how the process works your attitude will be in your control.

The tips that follow are all about improving your attitude by better understanding how others affect you, and helping you to positively affect the attitudes of those around you. The more you realize how your attitude is impacted, the easier it will be for you to improve it.

Praise for Peers

When you notice someone doing something well, let them know about it. This tip will help you to improve the attitudes of those around you. In turn, their good mood will help to boost your attitude.

The Company You Keep

The people around you have a major impact on your attitude. Negativity can spread, and fast. When you take part in conversations at work or at home that have a negative angle, you may soon find yourself joining in. Do your best to keep clear of negative conversations. This will help you to keep your positive attitude strong and growing.

✦ ✦ ✦

Negative Situations

When you are involved in a negative situation, and you realize you cannot improve upon it, leave. Simply excuse yourself politely and use your time for something more effective and worthwhile. One of the skills you will learn is to not only end your negativity but to avoid the negativity of others.

✦ ✦ ✦

Let Them Know It

If the negativity of others around you becomes an unavoidable problem, try bringing it up to them in a neutral manner. It is a very difficult task to bring up someone's negativity to them, but that doesn't mean you shouldn't do it. Keep in mind that you are doing so for their own good. A problem that goes ignored will only grow and cause more complications in the future.

✦ ✦ ✦

Are You Responsible?

Are you spreading negativity to others? You may have to think about this one when you are feeling especially understanding and positive. At the time of negativity it is difficult to be logical and unbiased. When the time is right, ask yourself if you are the one who is bringing the group down.

✦ ✦ ✦

Start with Good News

Before you get involved in conversations with other people, have a piece of good news to share. This will help you to start off conversations on the right foot. It may also help the other person to stay on the path of a positive talk.

✦ ✦ ✦

Exchange Negatives with Positives

When someone hands you a negative, be creative and hand them a positive. You have to be careful with this tip, because you could end up putting the other person on the defensive. Simply state your positive in a neutral way, without countering their negative statements. It takes tact to turn a conversation, but with enough practice you'll be a pro.

✦ ✦ ✦

Give a Helping Hand

When a close friend or family member is constantly looking at things negatively, help them out. It will be tough, and it may not work in the end, but it is well worth the risk. Having a negative attitude decreases the overall enjoyment of life. The more you can do to help those who see the world in a negative way, the better.

✦ ✦ ✦

What to do About Gossip

Gossip is dangerous. Not only is the tone negative and hurtful, it spreads twisted sto-

I don't like that man. I must get to know him better.

Abraham Lincoln

The Signal

Create a signal with your friend to use when one of you becomes negative. In some instances, it is easier to simply make a gesture to let them know they are negative rather than verbally telling them.

ries and threads of truth to unsuspecting individuals. If gossip comes your way, step aside and let it pass you by. Even better, put a stop to it if you can.

◆ ◆ ◆

Changing Your Group

Hopefully it won't come to this, but sometimes the only solution to eliminating negativity from your life is to make a change in the company you keep. If you have a friend who, after trying to help them, continues to bring negativity to every situation, you may have to move on.

◆ ◆ ◆

Move Your Work Station

If you are having trouble dealing with a particular co-worker, move your work station to a different area. This is a quick way to avoid their negativity.

◆ ◆ ◆

Work to Fix the Cause

Find the cause of the negativity and fix it. For example, if employees are upset with a particular aspect of the working environment make an effort to remedy the situation. This is a win-win situation for everyone. The negativity and frustration of your co-workers is alleviated and a problem in the work environment is solved.

◆ ◆ ◆

The Kind Listener

This may not be your intent, but some people seem to like the negative stories of others. If you are willing to listen to people complain,

and show an interest in their frustrations, they may look to you every time they are upset. This is fine if they are looking for support and advice. What isn't okay is a constant complainer looking for you every time something goes bad.

✦ ✦ ✦

The Power of One

One person, negative or positive, can shift an entire group depending on the the the person's strength of character and confidence. Put yourself in the role of attitude shifter.

✦ ✦ ✦

Praise the Positive

When a normally negative individual displays a positive attitude, give them sincere praise. If a negative individual receives positive feedback for being positive themselves, it will help to reinforce the good characteristics they have just shown. Positive reinforcement for a positive attitude.

✦ ✦ ✦

Your Vocabulary Affects Others

What words do you use on a daily basis? Do you use negativity to describe situations? If so, you may be passing a negative feeling from yourself to others. Pay attention to the words you use.

✦ ✦ ✦

Complaining at Work

Be careful not to complain too often. It is foolish to think that you will never complain or have bad days, but complaining can become a habit. This trait can cause negative feelings long after the talking has stopped. You will

Adopting the right attitude can convert a negative stress into a positive one.

Dr. Hans Selye

Ending on a Good Note

When attitudes collide, or a negative conversation is taking place, try to end on a positive. This will decrease the chances for hard feelings or grudges to be created.

also be spreading those negative sentiments to those around you. Stop complaining at work and you'll notice a definite improvement in your attitude.

✦ ✦ ✦

Reenacting Negative Moments

Do not reenact fights, conflicts, or negative situations to tell a story. This is a habit of many, many people. After they experience an upsetting event, they reenact that event and may cause further anger or frustration by doing so. It is good to talk things out, but when you reenact negative situations, you stir up the angry feelings again and may even put your listener in a bad mood.

✦ ✦ ✦

Do People Comment On Your Attitude?

Do those around you remark that you have a negative attitude? If they do, regardless of whether or not you agree, take action to reverse it. You may not want to admit it to yourself, but your friends and family will be less biased when it comes to you and your moods. Take their comments as a positive and begin the process of attitude improvement.

✦ ✦ ✦

You Can Affect Others

Not only can you change the direction of a conversation with positives, you can change the direction of someone's day, month, or even life with the right words and philosophies. Be an example for others to follow.

23

Top of Mind

I F IT'S NOT IN FRONT OF YOU, you may just forget it. The answer? Attitude reminders! A simple note here and there or a small message can go a long way in keeping your attitude just how you like it.

The pace of today's world is overwhelming. Everything was supposed to be done yesterday and today's to-do list reaches for miles and miles. In this hectic environment a small reminder will help to keep you aware of the greater goals.

Meanings

Attach meanings to objects in your environment. This will remind you to stay calm, in control, and positive even when things don't work out just right. Here are a few examples:

✧ a garden to remind you to stop and smell the flowers

✧ a child to remind you to have fun

✧ a phone to remind you to stay connected with friends and family

Calendars

We have been through calendars as reminders for goals, to get motivated, and now to keep your attitude going strong. The choices go on forever when it comes to calendar types, styles, and themes. They are a quick and easy way to give your attitude a pick-me-up. The most common choices are calendars with quotations, picturesque scenery, or artwork.

✦ ✦ ✦

Posters

An athlete has her role model on a poster on the wall. A scientist has a poster of significant advances in science and medicine on his wall. A teacher has a poster listing the lessons you learn in school on her wall. Find a poster that reminds you to stay positive and happy.

✦ ✦ ✦

Books

There are thousands of books out there about improving your attitude, maintaining your positive attitude, and helping others to do the same. If you find value in these books, keep one handy.

✦ ✦ ✦

Tapes

As with books, there are many tape programs that will help you with your attitude. If you would rather have someone listen to you instead of reading the words yourself, audio programs are the perfect solution.

✦ ✦ ✦

A Picture to Remember

Do you have a picture that affects you? A picture that makes you feel good? If so, don't file it away with your memories. Keep it out in the open as a reminder. Put it on your fridge, put it in a frame and place it on a table, or keep it taped up in your gym locker. It doesn't matter where you place your picture, just as long as you see it often.

✦ ✦ ✦

Write Yourself a Message

When you are in a great mood and nothing can keep you down, write a message to your future self. In this message, write down the reasons why you will not fail in whatever you try, why you will find a way to make things work, and the good things you have in your life. Keep the message close to you. When the time comes that you are down, read your message and take the advice to heart.

✦ ✦ ✦

The Wallet-Sized Attitude Adjuster

Place a quotation, message, word, or significant phrase on a small wallet-sized card. For durability, use heavier paper or laminate it. Keep this reminder in your wallet or purse. Whenever you are feeling like you are sliding towards the negative end of the spectrum, out comes your card to the rescue.

✦ ✦ ✦

Screen Savers

Either create a positive message yourself, or find one somewhere else. Use this message as your screen saver. When you are looking

There is nothing either good or bad but thinking makes it so.

William Shakespeare

Think Twice, Before You Act Once

Before you react to a problem, think twice. During this time you can remember all of the attitude lessons you have learned. After taking a breath and thinking logically you will be able to fix the problem in half the time.

for a reason to feel better, you may just look up from your desk, see your screen saver message scroll, and smile.

✦ ✦ ✦

Hello Me

In the morning, give yourself a quick pep-talk about what the rest of the day holds. Remind yourself of the lessons and tips you will try to use throughout the afternoon, and the positive attitude you will attempt to maintain into the evening. This will give you a running start for the next ten hours.

✦ ✦ ✦

Remind Yourself with Self-Talk

To remind yourself about keeping a positive attitude, use self-talk. We already know the benefits of using self-talk to create a desirable attitude, and now we are using it again to reinforce the message.

✦ ✦ ✦

Put a Poster on Your Ceiling

Want a great way to start and end your day on a high note? Put a poster on your ceiling directly over your bed. When you wake up in the morning, the first thing you'll see is a positive message. When it's time to hit the sack at the end of a long day, you will see the words of wisdom as you drift off to sleep.

24

Attitude at Work

YOUR JOB IS FILLED with responsibilities, co-workers, bosses, deadlines, and pressure to do things well, right, and on time. With the right attitude, work can be an exciting and satisfying experience. Because so much of your time will be spent working, it is important to have a winning attitude to help you succeed and also help others to reach their goals.

This chapter includes tips to help you keep your attitude positive in the face of workplace challenges. The road to the top is open to those who have the right attitude and skills. Soon, you will be well on your way to a smooth drive to the top.

Bulletin Boards

If there is space around the office, create a small bulletin board. On it you can post jokes, funny stories, successes of co-workers, employee of the month awards, or anything else that will perk up the office.

Don't Work Too Hard

You probably haven't heard this request too often, and with good reason. Overall, a great deal of individuals could stand to work a little harder, but in this respect, the key is to not overwork yourself. You may feel great about working without a break or breather, but your effectiveness may slowly start to decrease as your energy, focus, and responsiveness slip.

✦ ✦ ✦

The Extra Assignment

It happens to all of us. We have a full load of work on our plate, and in comes your friendly co-worker offering to pile on just a bit more. She could really use a favor, and needs your help. Sometimes you just have to say no. It is difficult, indeed, but it is necessary. When the responsibilities of others continue to fall on your lap, you may have to get used to saying a few more no's than you did previously. Politely explain to them that you don't have the time right now and must focus on your own responsibilities.

✦ ✦ ✦

Quitting Time

This is for the overachievers. Set a mandatory quitting time for yourself at the office. Many times work can take complete control of your life, leaving little room for other activities. Setting a time that you must stop working will ensure that you do not get too tense, stressed, or mentally and physically drained.

✦ ✦ ✦

The Delicate Balance

Striking a healthy balance between work and home has been a struggle for many men and women throughout the working world. The problem compounds when you are passionate about your work, and wish never to leave it. Working hard is a virtuous endeavor, but when it cuts into family and home, changes are required. For a truly happy life, you need both career satisfaction and the love and friendship of your family. Without the latter, the first will be of little consequence.

Good is not good where better is expected.

Thomas Fuller

✦ ✦ ✦

When at Home, Be at Home

Separating work and home can be a difficult thing to do. Deadlines to be met, projects to be completed, new challenges appearing around every corner. Many of us can't help but think about work responsibilities as we leave the office, drive home, and enter the front door. It may be difficult, but it will help to keep your attitude calm and your stress low. When the workday is done, the workday is done. As you drive away from the business, change gears and prepare your mind for home.

✦ ✦ ✦

When at Work, Be at Work

The other side of the coin is also very important. When you leave your home in the morning, afternoon, or night heading for your job, leave the issues at home where they belong. The idea is to focus on the task at hand, and not what is happening in another part of your life. It is difficult, to be sure, to keep your

Begin with a Hello

As soon as you walk through the front doors say hello to each employee that you see. Some workers have a habit of hanging their head as they stomp through the hallways. Not only does this affect your attitude but also the attitude of those around you. Begin your day in a positive way and you'll finish in just the same manner.

work and home life completely separated. But knowing the danger of mixing realities will help you to make informed decisions about how you work and live.

✦ ✦ ✦

Play Music While You Work

If possible, turn on the radio while you work to keep your energy up or to calm your nerves. The selection of music will be determined by the desired effect. Classical music would be a good fit for a stressful project or a situation where you must think calmly and in a relaxed state of mind. If you need energy, rock n' roll might be a better match for your needs.

✦ ✦ ✦

Create a Success File

Create a file at work for positive reviews, glowing reports, and other achievements you are proud of. This will help to improve your confidence and attitude whenever you need a quick boost.

25

Children & Attitude

I F YOU HAVE EVER WONDERED how you can improve the attitude of your children, you are not alone. Thousands of parents are looking for ways to raise kids with positive outlooks and winning attitudes. Once you realize that your attitude is under your control, it follows that the same is true for your children. Using the systems with your kids will help to give them the tools they need to succeed in the future.

This chapter offers you proven techniques to create an environment where your kids learn the importance of a positive attitude. One of the greatest lessons you can pass on to your children is the power of a positive attitude.

Bad Days

Everyone has bad days. This is important for your children to understand. If you teach them about having a positive attitude they may feel like they are failing when they aren't in a good mood. As long as the mood doesn't last long, being down now and then is natural and allowable.

Create a Bicker-Free Zone

Designate certain areas of the home as spots where fighting and bickering are not allowed. It would be ideal if the entire home were a place for this kind of program, but choosing several rooms will have a greater impact. For instance, the family room can be designated as a 'bicker-free zone' where siblings or moms and dads cannot bring negativity.

✦ ✦ ✦

Teach Them About Attitude

In many families, goals and motivation are not common subjects. That is a shame. Children will require these skills and characteristics as they grow older, but if the home does not teach these lessons, where are they to learn them? In most instances, they don't. Break the cycle and explain the importance of a positive attitude to your children from a very early age. This is one of the most important things you can pass on to your kids. Don't miss the chance to do so.

✦ ✦ ✦

Lead by Example

What you do your children see, think about, and in many cases, do as well. When you demonstrate a positive outlook on life, and bring a positive attitude to the situations you encounter, your children will learn from your example.

✦ ✦ ✦

Practice What You Preach

This old adage has seen it's fair share of lip service. We find that it is much easier to offer advice than to actually follow it. It may be difficult, but in order for your words of wisdom to sink into your children's heads, they must see you do what you tell them to do. You cannot talk with them about being responsible and then call into work with a fake excuse. Teach them the lessons they must know, and live those lessons yourself.

✦ ✦ ✦

Use Positive Reinforcement

Study after study has shown that positive reinforcement wins over negative reinforcement. When you see them doing something right, be sure to tell them about it. It's easy to fall into the trap of only noticing the problems or trouble that arises. By giving them positive reinforcement you will help them to develop confidence and self-esteem; two major building blocks of a positive attitude.

✦ ✦ ✦

The Sign that Reminds

Make a small sign to hang on your children's door. On it, write the words *Catch me doing something right*. This will remind you to see both the good and the bad that comes from your child. Hopefully you'll begin to see a lot more of the good once you put these tips into use.

✦ ✦ ✦

The Bigger Picture

What happens in the home has an enormous impact on your child's life and future. This alone does not complete the picture. The outside influences that affect your child may counteract several of the things you are try-

Too often we give children answers to remember rather than problems to solve.

Roger Lewin

The Goodnight Talk

After tucking your children in to bed, you have their full attention for any message that you want to impart. There are no distractions, no games, and no television. It's just you and your son or daughter. These are the times you can give advice about keeping a positive attitude and never giving up. You could also use your goodnight talks as a time for praise and encouragement. Let them know how proud you are, and how you know they will continue to succeed and grow as happy and healthy individuals.

ing to impart on them. Negative friends, for example, may cause a bit of confusion for your son or daughter. The solution lies in communication. Talk with your children about their friends and other influences. Educate them about the good and the bad influences that will enter into their lives.

✦ ✦ ✦

Their Attitude Outside the Home

A great attitude at home is a wonderful trait to have, but it may not be a perfect representation of the entire attitude. Does your child demonstrate a positive attitude at school with peers and teachers? How about with sports or other recreational activities? Make sure you understand how your child behaves outside of the home around others.

✦ ✦ ✦

The Parent Trap

I have personally spoken with many parents who simply could not accept that their children could ever do wrong. In their eyes, it had to be someone or something else. If a negative or bad attitude is the subject at hand, and you won't allow yourself to see it, there is trouble in your future. It is very difficult for parents to accept that their children aren't positive, friendly people. Overall, I'm sure the majority of children are, but the few instances of negativity cannot go unnoticed. Keep an open mind and an unbiased perspective when your children are in need of an attitude adjustment.

✦ ✦ ✦

Explain the Negatives of Negativity

For all of this talk of attitude to make sense, you may need to describe the negative outcomes of negative thinking. Each message will have to be tailored to the listener, but the key is to get across to them that there is a difference between being positive and negative, and that choosing the first is a much better choice in the long run.

✦ ✦ ✦

It's a Give to Get World

A negative attitude is like all other things in this world, if you give it, you get it. By treating others negatively, they will in turn do the same. If you treat others with respect, for the most part, they will treat you with respect. If you are positive towards your children, you will receive the same in return.

✦ ✦ ✦

Create Winning Opportunities

One of the most effective ways to improve the attitudes of your children, and to build their confidence and belief in their abilities, is to create situations for them to succeed. This includes tasks as simple as chores around the house, but also larger activities like schoolwork or accomplishments with athletics or music.

✦ ✦ ✦

Create Losing Situations

Sounds crazy, but it's a smart way to help your children learn how to fail. The creativity you bring to this tip is important, because a fine line must be walked between damaging their

Before I got married, I had six theories about bringing up children. Now I have six children and no theories.

John Wilmot

School Days

When your child comes home from school in a bad mood, your first impulse may be to tell your son or daughter to change their attitude. What you must remember is that children experience a great deal of self-doubt during their younger years. School days can be full of comparisons with other students, and challenges to their confidence and self-esteem. This may be the source of their mood swings. With a little talking you'll be able to get to the source and help them improve things.

confidence and improving it. Your children must learn that failing is okay, as long as they learn from that failure. Create a situation where they must first fail to ultimately succeed.

✦ ✦ ✦

The Attitude Test

Give your children hypothetical situations to see how they would respond. If they respond in a defeating or negative way, help them to see the other side of the picture. These simple examples will help your children to think in terms of opportunities and positives instead of problems and negativity.

✦ ✦ ✦

The Control is Theirs

The core principle of attitude is that the control lies with the beholder. No one can affect your child's attitude unless they let them. Ingrain into their minds that situations are neither good nor bad, only their thoughts make it so. We are not victims of society or environment. We control our perspective, attitude, and outlook. Your children are no different.

✦ ✦ ✦

Sleep-over Independence

A sleep-over for a young child is an excellent way to build independence and confidence. When the time is right, allow them to take part in these activities. It will put them in an unknown situation, and test their abilities to take care of themselves in a way that they have never had to before. With the safety nets all around (friend's parents, a phone call to home, etc.) it is a great way to build on the characteristics which will serve your children later in life.

✦ ✦ ✦

Creative Outlets

As I have mentioned before, creativity plays an intricate roll in motivation. Therefore, try to offer your children as many opportunities as possible to display and grow their creativity. Music is one of the most accessible and useful means of experimenting with creativity. The more outlets you can give your child, the more paths your son or daughter will have to develop an attitude that is interested in learning, growing, and improving.

Each day of our lives we make deposits in the memory banks of our children.

Charles R. Swindoll

✦ ✦ ✦

Drawing Supplies

Inexpensive and relatively mess-free, drawing supplies are an excellent outlet for your children to develop their creativity. You could keep it simple by giving them a pencil and paper, or add a little more zest to the project by including crayons, markers, construction paper, and any other supplies you think would be helpful. After a masterpiece is completed, up on the refrigerator it goes.

✦ ✦ ✦

Building Blocks to Build an Attitude

Building blocks are another inexpensive and effective way to allow your children to create and build. To make the activity more interesting, join in the fun. Sit down on the living room floor, with the television off, and help your kids play. Ask them what things they would like to

build, or why they are building a certain structure. The more you can get them thinking, and liking that process, the more they will see learning as fun and enjoyable.

Limit Television Time

"It's easy." While working with many parents of children who need more motivation, that is the excuse I hear the most for letting their kids watch television for prolonged periods of time. They're right. It is easy to drop them in front of the box and go about the rest of your day or night without a care in the world as to what or whom they are watching, or even worse, what that amount of television is doing to them mentally. In their excuse lies the answer. Most things that are worth doing are not easy to do. Only with time, effort, patience, and commitment do we feel the pride and sense of accomplishment we desire. It may take more work to create a positive learning environment for your kids in the home, but when it comes to their future, it's well worth it. Everyone must learn to do what is right, and not only what is easy.

Monitor Television Viewing

Be aware of what your kids watch on television. There are many educational programs offered throughout the day which will make a much better impact on your children than cartoons or violence and vulgarity. That does not mean that cartoons should be outlawed from the home. It simply means to make sure your children are able to learn from the programs on television, are not subjected to violence on television, and watch cartoons and other fun programs in moderation.

+ + +

Their Diet

A child's diet, just like yours, can affect their attitude, mood, and energy levels. They do, however, require different amounts of certain nutrients, vitamins, and minerals than adults do. After doing a little investigating, you'll be able to create a healthy and well-balanced diet for you and your kids.

+ + +

Sleeping Patterns

The bedtime may be ten o'clock, but that doesn't necessarily mean that they will fall asleep at that time. How many hours do your kids actually sleep? Do they wake up during the night? To find the answers you either have to be attentive to their sleeping patterns, or ask your kids directly. Either way, it is important for you to ensure that your kids are getting enough sleep. If it turns out that they are sleeping too much or too little, you may have found a source to a negative attitude.

+ + +

Firm but Fair

If they are displaying negative behavior, let them know it and also let them know that it is not acceptable. Allowing your children to get away with negativity now will make it nearly impossible to reverse that attitude later in life. You are shaping how they react or respond to situations and to life in general. Be sure to set boundaries and expectations for their character, personality, and attitude.

The soul is healed by being with children.

Fyodor Dostoevsky

I'm Home!

The first words you say when you enter your home are key to creating a positive atmosphere. If you start complaining about messes, homework, or chores before you say anything else you'll put everyone in the house in a defensive, negative mood. Instead, enter the home with warm greetings and smiles. Then you can get down to business.

Phone a Friend

The telephone is not only a way to communicate with others, but also a great tool for improving attitude. How? Having your children make phone calls is another step in building their independence and confidence, and this in turn leads to a healthy, confident attitude. This includes calling friends and family members.

Carry-Out or Delivery?

Another effective phone tip is to allow your kids to order dinner for delivery. Before the call is placed, go through the required information and make sure they understand the process. It may sound simple, but I have seen a smile come across a child's face when they hang up the phone. It takes small steps to produce large changes and improvements, and this is one small step to a more confident, positive child.

Have Your Children Ask for Help

When help is needed, let your children ask for it. For example, if you are in a grocery store and can't find the items you are looking for, ask your son or daughter to find an employee and ask for help. You should, of course, be in the immediate area.

Dinner Day

Create a dinner day for your kids. They decide what to have, and, with your help, make the meal for the rest of the family. You'll be surprised at what you get in the end, but hopefully it will be a pleasant surprise. After putting this tip to use in your home you may want to have these days separated a bit further if your kids have different tastes than the rest of the family.

✦ ✦ ✦

P.E.T.

Perpetually effective teaching. Giving your children the responsibility and accountability of a pet is an excellent way to give them hands on experience and a lot of fun. Be careful not to let the duties slip over to your table. All too often the cries of, "I fed him last week!" or, "It's not my turn to walk the dog," drive you crazy enough to do it yourself. Keep the responsibility on their shoulders, and you will be giving them priceless experience and confidence in their abilities.

✦ ✦ ✦

The Top-Ten List

For each child in the family, write out the top ten things you like most about them. Type them into a word processing program, print onto quality paper, frame, and hang in their rooms or family room. This small and simple process will speak volumes to your children. One of the keys to a positive and winning attitude is feeling valued and accepted. What better way than to give your kids a tangible reminder of how important they are to you.

✦ ✦ ✦

Children have more need of models than of critics.

Carolyn Coats

Smart Choices

State your thoughts in a positive way. This will teach your children to handle problems and unforeseen obstacles with a calm and positive attitude. If you burn dinner you could say, "That's just perfect, another problem," or, "Oops. Well, I guess we'll have something else instead." Keep it positive and they'll learn how to handle problems the smart way.

One of the Most Important Resources in the Home

Your refrigerator is the place to display the successes, accomplishments, and goals of your family. If you haven't already done so, purchase five to ten magnets. You can use promotional magnets that you receive from local businesses or small trinket magnets that you have collected over the years. If you want to take it a step further, you can purchase blank magnets and create your own messages on your home computer. Phrases such as "Great Job!", or "I Reached My Goal!" will have a greater effect when a paper, report card, or project is placed on the fridge.

✦ ✦ ✦

Let Them Ask for Directions

This one may take a little more supervision, but is effective just the same. When you are lost, or in need of directions, let them ask. If you stop at a gas station, follow them inside, stand near, and let them solve the directional challenge.

✦ ✦ ✦

Never Forget This

Simple words such as important, proud, and care are not only important for a successful upbringing, but very necessary. With all of the stress and hectic schedules parents face each day, it's easy to forget to tell your children how important they are and how much you care about them. Time restraints, however, are not valid excuses. Make time to let your children know you care, and they will do the same for you.

Target the Action, not the Actor

When your child, or anyone for that matter, does something wrong, discipline the action and not the person. For example, if one of your kids comes home with a failing grade, focus on the grade and solutions to improve it rather than seeing it as a failing child. This will make it possible for you to fix problems without creating negativity and defensiveness.

✦ ✦ ✦

Let the Little One Rule

If you have two or more children, it may be that the youngest one gets a rough deal now and then having to walk in the shadows of his or her older siblings. To remedy this problem, let the little ones be in charge sometimes. Let them choose what to have for dinner, or give them the easier chores around the house.

✦ ✦ ✦

Let Them Learn

When your kids are learning new things you may have the urge to jump in and help. In some instances, this is a good thing. There are times when your kids need your help, but there are also times when you shouldn't hover over them. Letting them learn without guidance is healthy and necessary for a strong, confident child.

✦ ✦ ✦

Talk About the Things You See Together

When you and your children view things together that are important, such as someone with a positive attitude or with a lot of moti-

> *You should study not only that you become a mother when your child is born, but also that you become a child.*
>
> *Dogen*

Attention Grabbers

Some children will carry a negative attitude solely to get attention. This doesn't mean that you should ignore their negativity. It is another possibility to factor into the parenting process. If you can't find a good reason for their moodiness, they may just be looking for more attention from you. If so, give it to them for positive actions and attitudes.

vation, talk with them about it. What do they think about the situation? The more you talk with your kids about the traits you would and wouldn't like them to have, the better their understanding will be. This can replace the "Because I said so," reasoning with solid facts as to why you want them to behave one way or another.

✦ ✦ ✦

Consequences to Actions

Another important aspect of attitude is accountability. Your kids must realize that their actions have impact on others. When they do something wrong, keep them accountable for their actions. If you run to the rescue and either deny the act or take the blame yourself, you'll be taking away an important learning experience from your kids. When they become accountable for their actions you will see a definite improvement in attitude.

✦ ✦ ✦

Have Them Call in Absences

When your son or daughter is going to be absent for school, sports, or other clubs/organizations, have them call it in. This should, obviously, be avoided when they are sick or unable to due to health reasons. If they will miss basketball practice because of a birthday party, let them call the coach. This is another way to teach your children to be responsible.

✦ ✦ ✦

It's the Thought that Counts

When your children are looking for gifts to give for holidays and birthdays help them to fully understand the meaning of giving. Let them know that choosing something haphazardly takes away from the present. It is the thought that counts, not the money or material gifts.

✦ ✦ ✦

Watch Movies that Demonstrate Giving

During a movie night with your family, choose a movie that has a central theme of giving. This is a lesson that your children should learn from a very young age. Helping your children see that they must give to get will go a long way in creating a healthy, happy, and positive child.

✦ ✦ ✦

Confidence Booster

Studies have shown that wrestling with your kids not only improves their relationship with you but also their confidence. Just when you thought rough-housing was bad, and now you have to join in the fun.

✦ ✦ ✦

The Fairy Tale System

Read fairy tales to your kids at night. The stories will teach them the difference between right and wrong, and help them to realize the value in doing what is right. It will also demonstrate to them the power of believing in yourself and in others.

✦ ✦ ✦

Close the Complaint Department

It is a common habit of many adults to come home after a long day at work and complain about what went wrong and what didn't go

Children are our most valuable natural resource.

Herbert Hoover

The Source of Negativity

When someone is negative they are not thinking illogically on purpose. At the time, they chose that attitude or reaction as their best option. Try to see the reasons behind their moods. This will help you to confront the situation with an understanding of their viewpoint. When you can relate to someone who is acting negatively it will go a long way to correcting the situation.

right. This may help you cool your nerves, but all of the negativity will affect your kids. Try to swallow your complaints for the good of your children, and talk about the positive things that happened throughout your day. Setting an example of constant complaining is an example you'll regret in the future.

✦ ✦ ✦

The Unscheduled Time

Most kids have a packed schedule with school, music lessons, sports, and other activities taking up the bulk of their time. Sometimes your kids just need some down time. When you are working out their weekly or monthly calendars, schedule in some time for them to relax and have time for themselves. Too much and too fast can lead to stress and tension that will cause major problems.

✦ ✦ ✦

School at Home

This may only work with the younger kids out there. When school is canceled, or you need an idea for an activity, play school. Have the older kids teach the younger kids what they are learning. You can use worksheets, tests, and textbooks. It's a great way to build their confidence and education on a day off.

SECTION FOUR
Online and Offline Learning

26

Maximizing Usage

T HERE IS MORE INFORMATION within your reach than ever before. Books, magazines, newsletters, Web sites, and other resource centers offer support and solutions for every problem you face. The problem isn't finding the information, it's in remembering and retrieving it.

This section will give you the tools you need to save useful information and quickly retrieve it. Information that gets lost in the clutter is of no use to you. When you take the necessary steps you will have the answers you need at your fingertips.

What Was That?

If you didn't understand a phrase or idea in your book go back and reread it. It isn't a race to the finish. Take as much time as you need to fully enjoy and understand your reading material.

Bookmark Your Favorites

When you come to a Web page that you find very helpful or interesting, bookmark that page or add it to your favorites. That way you'll be able to revisit with the click of a button.

✦ ✦ ✦

Directories

Use directories to find information. Directories are human-compiled guides to the web, where sites are organized by categories. The main difference between a search engine and directory is that a directory does not make use of indexing software and so has no way of knowing about a site if it's not submitted to them directly.

✦ ✦ ✦

Searching Tips

When you search for subjects on the Internet you can use a variety of methods that will retrieve very different results. For instance, if you search for a phrase such as, *positive attitude*, you'll receive different results than if you typed in, *positive + attitude*. Adding a plus sign between words or placing quotation marks before and after your phrases will help to narrow down your search. You can also try putting keywords in a different order. Be sure to use several different search engines to find information. Each engine uses its own system for retrieval, and a set of results from one search engine will not match that of another.

✦ ✦ ✦

Print Out Material

I have read a lot of great material on the Web, but I must admit that reading a large amount of text on the screen isn't easy on the eyes. When you are facing the same situation, simply print out the material you are interested in. It's easier to read, page through, and you can highlight or underline key areas and ideas.

◆ ◆ ◆

Network

When you need to find people who are in your field, occupation, or area of interest the Internet offers more opportunities than ever before. Millions of people are only a Web site away, and a quick e-mail is all it takes to get the communication started.

◆ ◆ ◆

Free E-Books

E-books, or electronic books, are everywhere on the Internet. Many of them, but not all, provide a lot of good content and are a great way to obtain free information. Keep your eyes open for free e-books, and you'll most likely come across a few that are worth reading.

◆ ◆ ◆

Discussion Forums, Clubs, Organizations

There are thousands of clubs and groups you can join on the Internet that are built upon the hobbies and interests that you love. All you need to do is look around and you're sure to find a group that fits your needs. If you are a work-at-home mom, take part in a forum discussion about that very area. If you are try-

Employ your time in improving yourself by other men's writings, so that you shall gain easily what others have labored hard for.

Socrates

Don't Say It

A common habit of readers is to mouth the words as they go along. This slows your reading speed considerably. Your eyes can process words much faster than you can say them. When you read, keep your mouth shut.

ing to lose weight or stop smoking, join an online support group for advice, tips, and motivation.

✦ ✦ ✦

Read with a Pen

Always have some type of writing instrument when you read. It will come in handy when you want to mark important sections, underline key thoughts, or write yourself reminders about how you will apply what you are learning.

✦ ✦ ✦

Highlight Key Passages

A highlighter is also a great tool to have when reading. You can really make important sections stick out for easy retrieval. The difference between the highlighter method and using a pen or pencil is simply personal preference. Either tool is effective.

✦ ✦ ✦

The Back Page

If you don't mind writing in your books to keep notes, try using the inside of the back cover. Most of the insides of back covers are completely empty and offer a nice amount of space for writing. Instead of searching for a scrap of paper when an idea hits you, you'll have everything you need right at your fingertips.

✦ ✦ ✦

When the Idea Hits You

I can guarantee that you will get new ideas and thoughts as you read books, magazines, newsletters, etc. As soon as that idea pops into your head, the next five minutes are critical. Why? Because if you do nothing to remember that idea, in five minutes it will most likely be gone. Don't let this happen to your ideas! As soon as you get a thought, write it down. Write it on paper, in the book, on a bookmark, anywhere you can.

✦ ✦ ✦

Speedy Reading

For faster reading, use your finger or a pen to underline the words as you go along. This will keep your pace constant and keep you from getting stuck in a rut.

Some books are to be tasted, others swallowed, and some few to be chewed and digested.

Sir Francis Bacon

APPENDIX
Resources

Foundation and Organization Contacts

FOUNDATIONS

The Salvation Army
101 Queen Victoria Street
London EC4P 4EP
United Kingdom
(703) 684-5532
www.salvationarmy.org

Goodwill Industries International, Inc.
9200 Rockville Pike
Bethesda, MD 20814
(240) 333-5200
contactus@goodwill.org
www.goodwill.org

March of Dimes
1275 Mamaroneck Avenue
White Plains, NY. 10605
(888) 663-4637
resourcecenter@modimes.org
www.modimes.org

Make-A-Wish Foundation of America
3550 N. Central Avenue
Phoenix, AZ 85012
(800) 722-WISH (9474)
mawfa@wish.org
www.wish.org

Muscular Dystrophy Association
3300 E. Sunrise Drive
Tucson, AZ. 85718
(520) 572-1717
www.mdusa.org
mda@mdausa.org

Boys & Girls Clubs of America
1230 W. Peachtree St. NW
Atlanta, GA 30309-3447
(800) 854-CLUB
www.bgca.org

Big Brothers Big Sisters of

America
230 North 13th Street
Philadelphia, PA. 19107-1538
(215) 567-7000
national@bbbsa.org
www.bbbsa.org

Special Olympics
1325 G. St NW, Suite 500
Washington DC 20005
(202) 628-3630
info@specialolympics.org
www.specialolympics.org

GET ORGANIZED

Post-It Notes
3M Center, Building 304-1-01
St. Paul, MN 55144-1000
(888) 364-3577
www.post-it.com

Get Organized Now!
PO Box 240398
Milwaukee, WI 53223-9015
getorgnow@wi.rr.com
www.getorganizednow.com

Franklin Covey Co.
2200 West Parkway Boulevard
Salt Lake City, UT 84119
(800) 654-1776
www.franklincovey.com

Mead
Courthouse Plaza Northeast
Dayton, OH 45463
(888) 795-2805
www.meadweb.com

Office Depot
2200 Old Germantown Road
Delray Beach, FL 33445
(888) GO-DEPOT
www.officedepot.com

Office Max
3605 Warrensville Center Rd.
Shaker Heights, OH 44122
(800) 283-7674
www.officemax.com

CONSTANT LEARNING

Toastmasters International
P.O.Box 9052
Mission Viejo, CA 92690
(949) 858-8255
www.toastmasters.org

Webster's Dictionary
Merriam-Webster Inc.
47 Federal Street
P.O. Box 281
Springfield, MA 01102
www.m-w.com

Bartlett's Famous Quotations
Bartleby.com, Inc., P.O. Box 13
New York, NY 10034
(646) 522-2474
bartlebycom@aol.com
www.bartleby.com

Discovery Channel
7700 Wisoncsin Avenue
Bethesda, MD 20814
(888) 404-5969
www.Discovery.com

A&E Television Networks
(212) 210-1400
www.historychannel.com
www.biography.com

Time Magazine
1271 Avenue of the Americas
New York, NY 10020
(800) 274-6800
www.time.com

National Geographic Magazine
1145 17th St NW
Washington DC, 20036
(800) NGS-LINE
www.nationalgeographic.com

USA TODAY
7950 Jones Branch Drive
McLean, VA 22108-0605
(800) USA-0001
www.usatoday.com

The New York Times
229 West 43rd Street
New York, NY 10036
(800) 698-4637
www.nytimes.com

Wall Street Journal
200 Burnett Road
Chicopee, MA 01020
(800) 568-7625
wsj.service@dowjones.com
www.wsj.com

Barnes & Noble, Inc
120 Fifth Avenue, 2nd Floor
New York, NY 10011
Phone: 212-633-3301
customerrelations@bn.com
www.bn.com

Amazon.com
P.O. Box 81226
Seattle, Washington 98108-1226
www.amazon.com

HEALTHY LIVING

Successories
2520 Diehl Road
Aurora, IL 60504
(800) 535-2773
www.successories.com

Ziglar Training Systems
2009 Chenault Drive
Suite 100
Carrollton, TX 75006
(800) 527-0306
info@zigziglar.com
www.zigziglar.com

National Sleep Foundation
1522 K St. NW, Suite 500
Washington D.C. 20005
(202) 347-3471
nsf@sleepfoundation.org
www.sleepfoundation.org

American Lung Association
1740 Broadway
14th Floor
New York, NY 10019-4374
1-800-LUNG-USA
www.lungusa.org

SEARCH ENGINES & DIRECTORIES

http://www.yahoo.com
http://search.aol.com
http://www.altavista.com
http://search.msn.com
http://www.excite.com

http://www.alltheweb.com
http://www.google.com
http://www.lycos.com
http://www.hotbot.com
http://looksmart.com